Sri Lank

CW00694603

The
Elusive Miracle of
Asia

Reflections on the passing scene – Religion,
Politics, Governance, Media and Personalities

By

Sharmini Serasinghe

*"I'd rather be downed for exposing the unjust
than praised and prized for shielding them!"*
– Sharmini Serasinghe

ISBN: 978-955-71371-0-0

Printed in United States of America

Lulu Press, Inc
627 Davis Drive, STE 300,
Morrisville,
NC, 27560-7101
USA

Dedication

To the future generations of Sri Lankans,
may you live to see the day the 'miracle' dawns!

Contents

Forewords

Daleena Samara

"Sharmini, your carriage has arrived," I announced. The guard room had called to say that Sharmini Dias Nagahawatte's ride was waiting to carry her home. Seated at the far end of the sub-desk near the boxy black telephone, I fielded most of the calls for the sub editors facing each other across the long line of desks in the open-plan office of the now defunct Independent Newspapers Ltd. We were a scruffy bunch, usually elbow deep in printer's ink. The words seemed appropriate: after all, Sharmini was the beautiful, impeccable princess in our midst.

It was the year 1982 and I was a sub editor at *Sun* newspaper and she an intern assigned to the *Op-ed* pages. We worked under the sharp eye of Rex de Silva, Chief Editor of *Sun* and *Weekend* and beloved mentor to us all. She was on a short internship for a journalism programme with the London School of Journalism. She had attended St Bridget's Convent, my alma mater. She was eighteen and I twenty-one. Embroiled in our own youthful worlds, we had little time for talk.

I left Independent Newspapers that year as did she. When we next met, it was online in the new millennium and we were continents apart. Sharmini invited me to join her Facebook group 'Mind on Matters', a stimulating forum of over a hundred members discussing subjects concerning the mind, religion, philosophy and politics, which exists today as 'Brainstormers Club'. Now in our fifties, both threshed in the mill of life, we were drawn together by a common thread – spirituality, in particular the Buddha Dhamma. She was a sincere practitioner of the teachings of the Buddha, as was I, albeit from the Mahayana stream. We exchanged notes and our friendship grew.

Sharmini had matured into a fierce, irreverent personality, unafraid to challenge norms and address controversies. She confronted the status quo, attracted foes, and made no apologies for kicking ass online. So, when invited to write a Personal Forward for her book, I thought to find out exactly how the metamorphosis had taken place. What made this only child of overprotective parents emerge from her gilded cage to stick her neck out so recklessly? Thirty-plus years ago, a doting father was picking her up and dropping her off at work, even accompanying her to interviews. He had sat in his car through her two-hour interview with Neville Kanakaratne, then Sri Lankan Ambassador to the United States, published as a centrefold spread in the *Weekend.* Rather than play safe in the security of her environment, Sharmini was going out on a limb to court trouble. What had happened in the years between

Independent Newspapers and now that had transformed her into an undaunted teller of uncomfortable truths?

Post-1982, Sharmini donned many hats, key among them being freelance journalist; programme producer and presenter for the Sri Lanka Broadcasting Corporation; English newscaster and editor, producer, director, presenter, interviewer, script writer of the State Television Sri Lanka Rupavahini Corporation and reporter for the *CNN World Report*; and Director Communications of the Government Secretariat for Coordinating the Peace Process in Sri Lanka (SCOPP). She was also wife twice over, mother, and more recently a grandmother. Her work had opened doors to a broad spectrum of events that slowly crushed her idealism and re-shaped her ideas, philosophy and character.

Particularly significant were her years with Rupavahini and SCOPP, which provided a window to the behind-the-scenes goings-on of the events of the day: the JVP insurrection, the war on terrorism, the scuttled peace efforts, the creeping nationalism, and the political corruption. In the newsroom at Rupavahini, she was privy to gruesome war footage that would never make it to our living room screens.

In 1989, when a freelance English-language newscaster at Rupavahini, she stood her ground when anonymous telephone callers claiming to be 'JVPers' ordered her not to read the news.

"Kill me if you want but don't insult me by thinking I'm a coward like you," she told them, with typical Taurean obstinacy. She continued to read the news, the only civilian, along with two officers from the Sri Lanka Air Force. She recalls that some viewers mistakenly suspected her of being a RAW agent of the Indian Peace Keeping Force who were fighting the LTTE at the time. Strangely, the anonymous calls continued at SCOPP, leaving her to speculate that they may have been initiated by an individual harbouring a personal grudge against her. When they came in the wee hours of the morning, she told the anonymous caller, "*Mawa maranna one nang maranna, habai karunakarala mage ninda maranna epa* (Kill me if you want to, but please don't kill my sleep)." The calls stopped thereafter!

Swept along with the tide of events sucking the country into an ever-deepening pit of darkness, Sharmini at first developed an immunity towards tragedy. Doing what most of us do, she put up her shutters and got on with her job. While freelancing at Rupavahini, she was offered a high-paying position of Manager Corporate Communications at tech firm, Virtusa. Six months later came a request from the newly-appointed Secretary General of SCOPP, Jayantha Dhanapala, former United Nations Secretary General for Disarmament, to join the Secretariat as Director Communications. After some hesitation, she agreed, seeing an opportunity to help the peace process and make a crucial difference to the country she loved.

She took massive pay and perks cuts to accept the position, where she worked alongside career diplomats and men of integrity such as Jayantha Dhanapala and Dr. John Gooneratne. But with the political regime change in 2005, she realised the futility of the new arena and watched her fragile dreams of much-needed peace fade in the face of mounting LTTE violations of the CFA, the sly manoeuvres of the Norwegian and other Scandinavian peace facilitators, and the gradual deepening of right-wing ideologies portending an ominous future. The events took their toll on Sharmini's health.

At the time, two key tragedies almost cost her, her life. The first was the assassination of the then Deputy Secretary General of SCOPP, Kethesh Loganathan, by the LTTE on 12 August 2006. Sharmini had spent that day working alongside her soft-spoken colleague. Aware that he was marked for death by the LTTE, her other colleagues were reluctant to share a car with him. But not Sharmini. That day, on a ride back from work with Loganathan, he asked her, "Why do you travel with me when the others don't want to?" She replied, "When it's time for me to die, I will, no matter whether it is in the car with you or somewhere else." That evening, Loganathan called her at home requesting some research. Hardly an hour later, she picked up the phone to answer a call from a colleague who asked: "Is it true? Is Loga dead?" Soon after her last telephone conversation with Kethesh, there had been a knock on his gate. As he opened it, he was shot through the head.

Incredulous at first, she rushed to the Kalubowila Hospital and asked to see the face of the corpse under the white sheet. Her worst fears confirmed, Sharmini broke down, weeping inconsolably. Days deadened with shock and grief followed. She began feeling numb in her limbs. Four months later, she resigned from SCOPP. Soon after, she collapsed with TIA (Transient Ischemic Attack or mini stroke). The hospital down the road made the difference between tragedy and recovery. Her fighting spirit kicked in and she was soon back on her feet. Kethesh Loganathan's death drove home an important lesson: "Stand up for what your conscience tells you is right, and also never take life for granted." In 2008, Sharmini returned to Rupavahini to work FOC as a producer of feature documentaries and co-host of the 15th SAARC Summit. She describes her years at the state television station – approximately twenty years in sum – as the "happiest in my life. The people I worked with were my family and what I was denied in my personal life, I was given in my professional life in abundance. And so, I wanted to give something back to Rupavahini. Though physically stressful, the work – especially the production aspect of it – was therapeutic." Her new series

'Discover Sri Lanka' was a winner with the viewers but she had to give it up due to interference by the management of Rupavahini at the time.

If I had thought Sharmini lived a charmed existence, I was wrong. The fine trappings of her sprawling childhood home, 'Sunny Side', and on Wicklow Hills Estate in Galle masked early years of pain. When she was just two and a half years old, her father, Mahendra Dias Nagahawatte, was severely injured in a motorcycle accident that sent part of a handle of the vehicle in through his stomach and out through the back missing his spine by inches. For the next ten years, the family home was consumed by his recovery. With her mother preoccupied with caring for her father, she was raised largely by servants and her grandparents. The next three years were spent with her maternal grandparents Seela Thalgodapitiya and Justice Walter Thalgodapitiya, in Kandy, where her grandmother's sister, Soma Kalawana, soon became her loving surrogate mother. It was from Justice Thalgodapitiya, the country's first Bribery Commissioner, also an author and Latin scholar, that she inherited the love for words and Latin.

When she turned five, Sharmini and 'Soma Athammi' moved back to Galle where Sharmini started her primary education at the prestigious Sacred Heart Convent. But although she enjoyed school, her mind was preoccupied with her father's health. He underwent over nineteen major surgeries in ten years, each an ordeal for the little girl who suffered nightmares about losing her beloved father. At age ten, Sharmini moved to Colombo with her family, and continued her education at Musaeus College.

At fourteen, recuperating in bed from a complicated surgery late one evening, Sharmini was confronted by a distraught teenage servant girl who thrust an empty bottle of insecticide at her, saying, "Tell Hamu I drank it." The suicidal girl was heart-broken over a love affair with the husband of the servant next door. Home alone with the girl that evening, Sharmini had the presence of mind to pick up a piece of paper and use it to take the bottle from the girl. Then, clutching her bandaged, still-raw wound, she stumbled to the house across the road and asked for help before collapsing on their doorstep. The girl was rushed to hospital but died the next day. In the aftermath, the family had to deal with scandalous reports falsifying the events of the suicide published in three different Sinhala newspapers.

During another particularly bleak phase, Sharmini, now a 25-year-old divorcee living with her five-year-old son and a domestic helper, had to contend with relentless interference for control of her life by immediate relatives. The scheming continued even after her marriage six years later, at age 31, to Hiran Serasinghe. Sharmini describes these events as "toxic manipulations" that turned her life into "a living nightmare", triggering a serious depression that included three failed suicide attempts.

But in life, it is not the hand that is dealt but how you play it that matters. Sharmini resurfaced from the miasma, a winner, stronger than before. She says now, "It was sheer grit – I am a survivor. I kicked out the negative, defeatist thoughts that had taken hold of me, refocused on my work and began writing." She attributes this resolute spirit to the influence of her formidable paternal grandmother, Jane Charlotte Dias Nagahawatte, who was widowed in her thirties while pregnant with her seventh child. She went on to quadruple the extent of her late husband's 250-acre tea estate Wicklow Hills, purchase St. Therese Estate in Nuwara Eliya, and build and buy mansions in Colombo for all her seven children. She was also President of the Low Country Tea Planters Association, the first and only woman to occupy the position to date.

By 2009, the country was suffused with the culture of fear and whispers. Threats of 'white-vanning' and the torture and disappearance of media personnel were increasingly common. The events of the morning of 8 January 2009 were perilous for Sharmini. When an SMS News Alert brought word of the murder of close friend and former colleague Lasantha Wickrematunge, she collapsed. This time, it was a serious stroke. It was months before she made a full recovery, regaining completely the use of her limbs, and her speech and memory, which the doctors said was nothing short of a miracle. That's when Sharmini began writing for publication.

Having witnessed death, courted death, and had death court her, she threw caution in the wind. Whereas she had been journalling for therapy after her depression, she now wrote furiously for the public. The words gushed out in anger in black on white to make peace with what she could not control. Words are a gamble, but they are powerful. What words reveal can create or destroy. Perhaps through writing, things could be done differently, hopes and dreams could be revived, and the dark soul of the country be reborn in the light. In doing so, she stepped forward as the voice of a majority silenced by fear of reprisal.

True courage comes from caring. Sharmini has a deep love for the Dhamma. In recent times, she has created two new Facebook groups on the topic *Sinhala-Buddhist Culture: An Insult to the Philosophical Buddha* with the goal of realigning the Practice with the true Path. Her personal essays in this book are revelatory of the disastrous erosion of the Dhamma by the politicisation of Buddhism and the resultant damage to the country and its peoples. Between the lines is a plea for sanity to prevail and the raising of the Dhamma and Sri Lanka out of the swamp in which it is now mired. The Buddha himself advised devotees to question the

Practice if they had concerns, and Sharmini is doing this unpleasant but necessary examination for Sri Lanka.

- Daleena Samara

John Gooneratne

I had seen Sharmini Serasinghe on TV News programmes and was familiar with her name and picture. But I had not met her. It was only when she joined the Peace Secretariat as Head of the Communications Division that I came to know her as a person. After a few preliminary exchanges, we were able to address each other as "Sharmini" and "John".

For a government office, something unusual about the Peace Secretariat atmosphere was that it was non-hierarchical. Each one knew his or her work, and there was no superior level officer who would be the supervisor. Officers would often consult each other. This helped one to respect each other's work.

A by-product of this was that even after we left the Peace Secretariat many years ago, we have continued our friendships made at the Peace Secretariat. Some have even formed WhatsApp groups.

As Sharmini and I continued our work at the Peace Secretariat, and as she occasionally consulted me, I could notice the different ways we looked at issues. She was a journalist, and as such would want to know what exactly happened and describe events as such. That would form the basis of whatever she would put into her writings and programmes. And this was how she looked at her work at the Peace Secretariat. I, on the other hand, had been a diplomat for over thirty years. And the approach we took would be different. While we diplomats also wanted to know what had happened, we would not necessarily always want to project it. We would, as circumstances demanded, often lie, shade or hide events on behalf of the State. So, lying, shading and hiding was something we could do on behalf of the State. I could thus see what was at the bottom of certain positions on which Sharmini would disagree with me.

Both at the Peace Secretariat and after, we on occasion discussed ongoing political developments. After all, at the Peace Secretariat we were close to the political decisions being taken. And after she left the Peace Secretariat, Sharmini continued her writing to newspapers and websites on the politics that was going on in the country and the personalities involved. And she would, on occasion, discuss such subjects with me. We exchanged views.

She is always wanting to find out what actually happened and show it to the reader. She will not accept lying, shading or hiding in her writing. And this is the approach that Sharmini takes in describing and assessing the subjects covered in her book.

-   ***John Gooneratne***

Jayantha Dhanapala

A few months into 2004, I had just returned to Sri Lanka after my five-year tenure as United Nations Under-Secretary-General for Disarmament Affairs in UN Secretary-General Kofi Annan's Senior Management Team. I received a call to meet President Chandrika Bandaranaike Kumaratunga, whose Coalition had been narrowly elected in the Parliamentary Elections. I was invited to assume the leadership of the Secretariat for the Co-ordination of the Peace Process (SCOPP) established to implement and co-ordinate the controversial ceasefire agreement (CFA) signed in 2002 between the Liberation Tigers of Tamil Eelam (LTTE) and the then Government of Prime Minister Ranil Wickremesinghe.

To some it appeared that I was being offered a poisoned chalice so fiercely was the CFA criticized for polarising an already fragmented nation; to others it was a challenge to maintain some continuity in the Government policy of peace-making in a decade or so of bitter and bloody conflict. I had my own reservations about the absence of balanced undertakings in the Ceasefire Agreement and the role of the Scandinavian-staffed Ceasefire Monitoring mechanism. But the congruence of policy on continuing the ceasefire and the respite it gave a weary nation had to be welcomed.

And so I took up the challenge, having cleared my doubts in a frank discussion with the Head of State, especially about her clarity of purpose in reaching a peaceful settlement. I set out to reform the structure of SCOPP, grateful for the valuable expertise I was inheriting with Deputy Secretary General Dr. John Gooneratne. Creating an effective Media Division, Economic Affairs Unit and Legal Affairs Division were vital priorities which occupied my attention while the LTTE prevaricated on finding an agreed formula for the resumption of negotiations. The media scene had changed in Sri Lanka. Journalists now played an overt political role inventing news and unashamedly plugging a point of view. I consulted a wide group for names for a possible head of the Media Division and, after interviews, Sharmini Serasinghe was appointed.

SCOPP was primarily a coordinating and facilitating body. It was the main instrument of the Government to consolidate and strengthen the peace process. The secretariat engaged in extensive consultations with all stakeholders involved in the peace process, including the public and private sectors, civil society, donor community and line agencies on a regular basis.

Its main areas of focus were to help implement Government decisions on the peace process, monitor the ceasefire agreement between the Government and the LTTE, provide research and logical support to the Government during political negotiations and to the National Advisory Council on Peace and Reconciliation, coordinate with local and international organizations on matters pertaining to the peace process, monitor the free movement of people and goods to and from uncleared areas, and communicate information about the peace process to media organizations and the public.

SCOPP officials were drawn from both private and public sectors and included specialists in communications, diplomacy, economics, and law who engaged in extensive talks with all the parties involved, which included representatives of the public and private sectors of the economy, civil society, charitable organisations, and line agencies.

The tasks of the Communications Division which Sharmini headed included monitoring and coordinating with local and foreign media organizations in dispersing information about the peace process, guiding and assisting non-governmental organizations (NGOs) and international non-governmental organizations (INGOs) in communications-related programmes on the peace process, and supporting other SCOPP divisions in communications-related matters. SCOPP already had its website 'Peace in Sri Lanka' in English and Sinhala up and running but not its Tamil version. After Sharmini took over as Director Communications, she and her team launched the Tamil version of the website. It was a first because at the time, even the LTTE Peace Secretariat didn't have their website in Tamil.

Also, under her purview an island-wide child art competition was conducted by SCOPP in collaboration with the Peace Education division of the Ministry of Education. This turned out to be a great success. We even received entries from children in rebel-held territory. With the six winning entries, SCOPP printed thousands of desk calendars (not with the tax payers' money) in Sinhala, Tamil and English, which were distributed island-wide.

During my tenure as SCOPP Secretary General, Sharmini and her counterparts from the other divisions of the Secretariat accompanied me on my numerous visits to Jaffna, Vavuniya, Trincomalee, Batticaloa, Mannar and Ampara where the District Offices of the SLMM were located. We interacted with the people of all these districts, including civil society, religious heads the armed forces, resettlement camps etc.

UN studies have shown that half of the number of countries emerging from conflict lapse back into conflict after around five years. This is precisely what happened in Sri Lanka. Though the UPFA Government under the leadership of President Chandrika Bandaranaike Kumaratunga spared no efforts in reviving the peace process and worked intensely to recommence peace negotiations, we had little to no success. The failure to recommence peace negotiations was primarily due to the fact that the LTTE was insisting that its demand for an Interim Self-Governing Authority (ISGA) should be the sole agenda item in the following round of talks.

The Government was willing to discuss all proposals for an interim authority as a prelude to a final settlement based on the Oslo Communiqué signed by the two parties on 5 December 2002, which agreed to explore a solution based on a federal structure within a united Sri Lanka. The Government however did not succeed and got the impression the LTTE was not interested in further discussions.

In my speeches at SCOPP, I was guilty of excessive use of an ancient Chinese proverb: "The more you sweat in peace, the less you bleed in war." I was rightly teased about it by my SCOPP colleagues but that is precisely what we did. The LTTE paid a heavy price in 2009 for failing to grasp the opportunity they were given. I am grateful to Sharmini and her colleagues in SCOPP for the unique esprit de corps within SCOPP and the professionalism of their work for the national cause. That professionalism and the sincere and fearless dedication to principle is evident in the pages of this book.

In my view, all transitions whether from insecurity to security, from war to peace, or from poverty to economic growth, are rarely smooth and stable. Political transitions are fraught with competition, controversy and tension. Economic transition can exacerbate inequalities, social transitions may exclude and marginalise some groups. We must therefore ensure that transitions are managed wisely and effectively.

- *Jayantha Dhanapala*

Preface

"By three methods we may learn wisdom: First, by reflection, which is noblest; second, by imitation, which is easiest; and third by experience, which is the bitterest." – Confucius

Upon reaching midlife and taking stock of my life, I can quite confidently sum it all up with the third: *"By experience, which is the bitterest."*

As with most of those of my generation, I have known mostly war, bloodshed, communal and religious intolerance. As a child of a single-digit age, I was in the thick of the bloody JVP insurrection of the '70s in Galle and carry vivid memories of this period even today. Not too long thereafter came ugly July '83; I was twenty years old. Somewhere in between, my schoolmates and I were segregated according to our ethnic labels. By this, we were forced to become aware of our 'differences' at a very tender age.

Along the way, I recall my mother constantly complaining about bread queues, fabric smelling of kerosene and almost anything and everything being rationed. I also remember my parents having to 'pull strings', grease palms and creep through back doors to obtain the requirements of my annual school booklists.

That more or less sums up my childhood. Now as a middle-aged Sri Lankan, I'm still searching for the much-trumpeted but thus far elusive 'Miracle of Asia – Sri Lanka'. I envy those who lived before me in the not-so-'miraculous' days of our country. It had to be far better than this!

So, whilst waiting with fervent hope and anticipation for the day this elusive miracle dawns, I decided to write this book which was a mere pipe dream until January 2015, when we Sri Lankans were set free from the tyranny of a megalomaniac political regime – for no publisher in their right mind would ever have agreed to publish it!

During those dark days of 2007, after the country was returned to the much-dreaded war, I returned to writing; my long-neglected passion. My morale had sunk to the lowest of lows. Here's why:

The fourth phase of the armed conflict between Sri Lanka's armed forces and the LTTE had commenced in July 2006; and so, in December that year, I resigned from the post of Director Communications of the Secretariat for Coordinating the Peace Process (SCOPP). I didn't see any purpose in working for a dead Peace Process, and SCOPP had ceased to serve its purpose in the face of a raging war.

This seemingly ceaseless war had been part and parcel of my life since the age of twenty. Working for the State Television, Sri

Lanka Rupavahini (TV) Corporation, as Guest Producer, newscaster, interviewer etc., brought its realities closer to home as I was privy to information and video footage so utterly gruesome, it was either heavily censored or never aired. The general public never saw what I saw behind the screen and hence couldn't have possibly felt what I felt. I lived it day in and day out for almost thirty years!

At the time I joined SCOPP in 2004, there seemed to be a near-tangible ray of hope for peace in Sri Lanka. I had utmost confidence in President Chandrika Bandaranaike Kumaratunga's sincerity in bringing about a lasting peace for our country. With eminent personalities from our foreign service, such as Jayantha Dhanapala, Dr. John Gooneratne and H. M. G. S. Palihakkara, to advise her, the sacrifice I made professionally and financially seemed well worth it. It was indeed a gamble, but one that I regarded as my contribution towards an eventual lasting peace in my country.

My respect for President Chandrika Bandaranaike Kumaratunga knew no bounds when in 2004, she issued a public national apology to the Tamil people of Sri Lanka for all the injustices they faced during the ethnic riots of July 1983. No leader before or after her had the decency or the courage to do so!

As the war raged on with no end in sight post-2006, I lost all hope. I had lost out on my gamble. Sheer disgust of the lows SCOPP dropped to after the Rajapaksa regime took over made me resign from my post as Director Communications. The only genuine pearls amidst the mass of fakes at the time were Foreign Minister Mangala Samaraweera and a lady I have the highest regard for, Madam Ferial Ashraff. Alas, they were about the only genuine participants outside of SCOPP in the Peace Process post-2005, amidst many charlatans.

SCOPP worked hand in hand with the Ministry of Foreign Affairs and its minister at the time, Mangala Samaraweera, who was beyond brilliant at his job. I personally regard him as a 'Lee Kuan Yew' Sri Lanka very desperately needs at this juncture and sincerely believe he's our only hope to turn our country around!

The first time I met the much-celebrated Jayantha Dhanapala, the former UN Under-Secretary-General for Disarmament and Sri Lanka's official candidate for the post of Secretary-General of the United Nations, and the distinguished career diplomat Dr. John Gooneratne at SCOPP, I referred to Mr. Dhanapala as "Dr. Dhanapala", and he gestured to his Deputy, Dr. John Gooneratne, and said, "He's the real doctor, not me". Such men of *éclat* and true *savants* but yet so humble!

Thereafter, during my first few days at SCOPP, I started referring to Dr. John Gooneratne as "Dr. John" like most others did until the day he told me, "If you continue to call me Dr. John, I will start calling you Mrs. Sharmini"; from then on, John became "John" to me.

As Director Communications, I found dealing with John, the Deputy Secretary General, extremely challenging, to put it mildly. Most of the time he was ever so endearing, but utterly frustrating to deal with when it came to official matters relating to the Peace Process. Even though he never refused to answer a question, the jargon he dished out was so convoluted that it left me totally confused and unable to remember the question I had originally asked, which was precisely his intention. All my media colleagues who had to deal with John will agree with me; you couldn't get anything out of the man!

Just listening to him speak on subjects other than the Peace Process, however, was an educating experience. But he zipped up on the Peace Process; his lips were practically sealed on the subject, which he was totally *au fait* with, having been involved with it since the day the Cease Fire Agreement (CFA) was signed between the LTTE and the Government of Sri Lanka in February 2002, and having attended all rounds of Peace Talks with the LTTE as a member of the Government delegation. He didn't reveal

28

anything to anyone except those who mattered; his long years of experience as a diplomat showed. When I eventually realised the reasons for his reticence, my respect for him knew no bounds!

I recall Secretary General Jayantha Dhanapala once telling me how heavily he depended on John for advice when making comments and decisions on the Peace Process. He also told me that John's wry sense of humour and his perceptive questions were a great asset in dealing with the sly Norwegian facilitators and that he often enjoyed his role of 'good cop' while John played bad cop, in typical John-style!

After Jayantha Dhanapala's resignation from SCOPP in November 2005, John was appointed Secretary General of SCOPP in December 2005, based on a Cabinet decision of the Government of Sri Lanka. But five months later, in May 2006, he resigned, much to the detriment of the Peace Process!

During his brief tenure as Secretary General, John was a force to reckon with and continued his role of 'bad cop' towards the Norwegian facilitators and the Sri Lanka Monitoring Mission (SLMM). I was privy to meetings at which more often than not John would let fly at them, while all his 'colleagues' backed him to the hilt.

Back during Jayantha Dhanapala's tenure at the helm of SCOPP, there were three designated spokespersons: the Secretary General,

Deputy Secretary General and the Director Communications (yours truly). Both Mr. Dhanapala and I communicated with the local and foreign media whenever there was something worthwhile mentioning, but from dear John, they got nothing. I would spend sleepless nights whenever Mr. Dhanapala was away from the country, because John simply refused to answer questions from the media and the onus was on me to do so.

Each morning, I would go to John's office to find out the 'media line' for the day, and his classic response was "what media line? Just give the usual one, men", which invariably meant 'outsourcing' the responsibility of answering the questions to the numerous self-appointed spokespersons in the Government on the Peace Process who were forever contradicting each other and leading the media up the garden path.

I later discovered that this was one of the main reasons John was so reluctant to speak on the subject to the media. Being a true intellectual on the subject, John didn't want to utter a word, and inevitably contradict the theories of the self-appointed Government pundits. My heart went out to my media colleagues and thanked my good karma for not being one of them at the time.

Being within the 'establishment', we had the advantage of knowing exactly what was and was not happening; and more often than not, we used to come across various hypothetical references to the

Peace Process in newspaper articles and reports, which the poor readers swallowed hook, line and sinker.

A stark case in point I recall was a reputed and respected weekly column regarded as 'highly credible' that reported on 'situations'. The writer/reporter quoting his 'very reliable, highly-placed source', went on to describe a high-profile meeting believed to have taken place at the Foreign Ministry. The author had even mentioned by name all those who were supposed to have been at this meeting and given a lengthy description of what had been discussed. The date and the time of the meeting were also mentioned. What he didn't know was that he had been taken for a right royal ride by his 'source' because the meeting was fictional and thus never took place as each and every person associated with it was out of the country at the time, bar John who was very comfortably seated behind his desk at SCOPP!

Although an internationally renowned career diplomat, the unassuming John used to travel to SCOPP and back home to Kottawa by bus, until Director Administration and Finance, H. D. Ariyaratna, insisted that he use an official vehicle. After all he was our Secretary General!

I must also mention that Secretary General Jayantha Dhanapala who served SCOPP *pro bono*, accepted the use of an official vehicle. However, out of a fleet of luxurious limousines to pick

31

from, what did he choose? A ramshackle apology for a car that had seen better day's decades before!

Under the leadership of Jayantha Dhanapala and Dr. John Gooneratne, a sense of *esprit de corps* prevailed at SCOPP. These two simple and unassuming gentlemen referred to all their subordinates as 'colleagues' and inspired us to work with sheer dedication to bring peace to our strife-torn Sri Lanka. We were not mere paper pushers but did our job out on the field. Frequent visits to Jaffna, Vavuniya, Trincomalee, Batticaloa, Mannar and Ampara where the District Offices of the SLMM were located were a norm. We interacted with the people of all these districts, including civil society, religious heads, the armed forces, and resettlement camps.

I must mention here that visiting the Peace Village, a resettlement camp located in the high-security zone in Jaffna, the brainchild of the then Security Forces Commander, Major General Susil Chandrapala, was an experience to behold. This man, a soldier, was a true man of peace! These were the unpretentious gentlemen; the *prominenti* I had the privilege of interacting and working with at SCOPP!

We also achieved some worthy successes for the Peace Process, although some of them turned out to be futile later on; the Post Tsunami Operational Management Structure (P-TOMS), negotiated and signed by the Government of Sri Lanka and the

LTTE, was one. This was the first time an agreement of its kind was signed on a functional subject. But we all know what happened to that one; the Supreme Court put paid to it.

Amongst the success stories was the Economic Affairs Division of SCOPP, headed by Seneka Abeyratne and his Deputy Director, Dr. Rajith Lakshman. They exemplified their dedicated contribution to the Peace Process through a well-researched and informative document titled *Impact of the Ceasefire Agreement on Regional Economic Growth in Sri Lanka.* It was quoted widely by the donor community as well as local researchers, as it was the only paper to provide sound empirical evidence of a significant economic dividend in the conflict-affected areas of Sri Lanka during the post-CFA period.

The solid contribution of the Economics Division, which of course went beyond this document, also engaged the private sector, Chambers of Commerce and the Multi-lateral Investment Guaranty Agency (MIGA). Seneka Abeyratne and Rajitha Lakshman provided solid analytical support to Secretary General Jayantha Dhanapala in addressing the various economic dimensions of peace.

I must mention here how the team effort of the Operations Division of SCOPP, under the leadership of Major General Sanath Karunaratne, and subsequently Major General Deepal Alwis, skillfully managed to coordinate the 'safe passage of LTTE cadres' be it on land, sea or air. This of course was in keeping with the true spirit of the CFA, which was *sine qua non* to the Peace Process. They ensured 'safe' transportation of LTTE terrorists for medical treatment in Colombo. They were also 'safely' flown to the Colombo International Airport, whenever they decided to talk and sometimes not talk. They were also 'safely' flown back from the Colombo International Airport to Tiger-held territory, whether they talked or not.

I also recall that soon after the havoc caused by the tsunami in December 2004, all of us at SCOPP collectively gathered food, clothing, medicine etc., and sent it to the LTTE Peace Secretariat in Killinochchi via the SLMM, as a gesture of goodwill. In return, what did we get from the LTTE? Egg in the face: they killed our Foreign Minister Lakshman Kadirgamar and our beloved colleague Kethesh Loganathan amongst many others.

The CFA, which was intended to be a platform for 'a negotiated political solution to the ongoing ethnic conflict' did not achieve its goal, but seemed to have suited the LTTE objectives to a T. The Government at the time was caught between the devil and the deep blue sea, being in the doldrums having suffered enormous military setbacks and a weak economy.

Many were the frustrations and drawbacks we had to live with in trying to tame the devious LTTE, which violated the spirit of the CFA with impunity while all we at SCOPP could do was change the adverbs in the 'condemnation template' which began: "The Government condemns/strongly condemns/unreservedly condemns/vehemently condemns/condemns in the strongest possible terms the killing of . . ." and dish out media releases which the LTTE could not care two hoots for.

There were many out there among the general public who regarded SCOPP as some sort of an institution mandated to mollycoddle the LTTE. One can hardly blame them given the fact that we were most of the time bending over backwards while trying not to appear to be doing so, to appease the cold-blooded LTTE.

The Peace Process also proved to be a very lucrative source of income for some. With the signing of the CFA, Non-Governmental Organizations (NGOs) mushroomed and some even tried their best to legitimize their overloaded wallets through SCOPP. They came up with such ludicrous ideas in the name of peace! The workshops on peace that these NGOs conducted in five-star hotels attracted a fair number of people, most of whom left midway or fell asleep after a sumptuous lunch. Eminent personalities from the international and local arena, specializing in 'Peace Making/Peace

Building', were frequent visitors to SCOPP. A few spoke on matters with substance and the rest spoke a lot but said nothing.

The CFA was seen by many as the last straw for an ever-elusive negotiated settlement to the ongoing conflict. However, flawed, it had benefits that were not visible to many. The euphoria was short-lived, and the rest is history.

The post-November 2005 Presidential election saw a sharp escalation in violence, with both signatories violating the agreement at will. Some of the more extremist coalition partners of the then ruling Government started demanding the abrogation of the CFA and the dismissal of the Norwegian facilitator. With the CFA practically sacrificed at the altar of short-term political gain, those of us who suffered and sacrificed much for the sake of a permanent peace in Sri Lanka could only sit back and wonder, was it all for nothing?

Post SCOPP, I decided to put my frustrations down in writing. They were very, very harsh despite my dear friend and former boss John doing his utmost to calm me down and prevent me from being 'White Vanned'. John has proved to be an indispensable pillar of strength and wisdom to me ever since I returned to my first love   writing. Thank you, dear Sir.

I'm also grateful to the Editor of *Colombo Telegraph*, Uvindu Kurukulasuriya, my dear friends D. B. S. Jeyaraj, and Editor of

Daily FT, Nisthar Cassim, for their courage to publish my articles unedited.

Many threats and warnings of 'White Vans' went over my head, as I was now ready to say what I had to say; do or die! Many who read my articles assumed I had fled overseas in fear for my life, hence the pluck to write what I did. But I felt neither fear nor the need to flee my country. I was right here in Sri Lanka throughout. I wanted my grandchildren to remember me as a woman who died screaming for justice rather than a coward with her mouth shut!

In this book, I make references to 'Sinhala-Buddhists' in a not a very complimentary manner. To me, the term 'Sinhala-Buddhist' represents one who follows and worships a superficial 'Buddhist culture' customs, idols, images, nonsensical traditions, while upholding an ideological rationale to legitimize ethnic majoritarianism, violent marginalization of minorities, oppression etc., thus hindering national security and development, peace and reconciliation in the country. I also refer to Mahinda Rajapaksa and his vile Sinhala-Buddhist ideology as well as his cohorts, including those men swathed in saffron robes masquerading as Buddhist monks, in a manner that might be construed as disparaging.

I refer to his ideology and culture-based mutation of the Nobel Teachings as 'Sinhala-Buddhism' or 'Cultural Sinhala-Buddhism' and practitioners as either 'Sinhala-Buddhists' or 'Cultural Sinhala-Buddhists', as opposed to the philosophy of peace that is the Dhamma, henceforth referred to as 'Philosophical Dhamma' or 'Philosophical Buddhism', with practitioners being 'Philosophical Buddhists'.

Facts are stubborn. The obvious tin-pot dictatorship of the Rajapaksa-era marked a new low in this country's history by merging Buddhism, the hapless Sinhalese, and the Sinhala-Buddhist Rajapaksas themselves, in an unenviable drama. The apparent induction of the 'State religious police', the Bodhu Bala Sena (BBS) led by Galagoda Aththe Gnanasara and his ilk, to promote, preach and propagate their own anti-Dhamma, a bigoted and venomous ideology, resulted in an attack on not only the Other, but on all moderate Philosophical Sinhalese-Buddhists.

All this happened under the very noses of the self-appointed 'guardians' of Buddhism in Sri Lanka; the Prelates of the Malwatta and Asgiriya chapters of the 'high-caste Radala and Govigama' Siam Nikaya. Yet they chose to look the other way. For this, history will remember them as those who contributed towards blasphemy of the revered Philosophical Dhamma!

Mahinda Rajapaksa will undoubtedly go down in history not as the hero who defeated LTTE terrorism but as one who reduced Sri Lanka's image from a country regarded as the cradle of Theravada Buddhism to a despotic and bigoted State governed by racist Sinhala-Buddhist fanatics.

Throwing caution and principles to the wind, self-described Buddhist Mahinda Rajapaksa and his cohorts embraced all that is ugly in his Sinhala-Buddhist toxic political ideology, using and abusing Buddhism to the maximum. I wonder if they realise how karma works!

Unlike his predecessors who made tactical use of Sinhala-Buddhism for political gain, Rajapaksa created a blatant political culture of the most oppressive, destructive and vicious strain of Sinhala-Buddhism, similar to the Al-Sauds of Saudi Arabia and their fanatical and primitive mindset of *Wahhabism*!

The Cultural Sinhala-Buddhist 'holy book' is the *Mahavamsa*. Hence it has been the 'bible' of the likes of Mahinda Rajapaksa since time immemorial. I have therefore referred to his mindset and those of his 'followers' in Chapter 9, *Mahavamsaism   The Scourge of Sri Lanka.* This 'holy book' of the Cultural Sinhala-Buddhist has made a mockery of the revered philosophical teachings of the Buddha and distorted it into a venomous and socially retrogressive political tool for ignorant Sinhala-Buddhists.

Thus, the *Mahavamsa* is revered by all those bigoted Cultural Sinhala-Buddhists whose base instinct is hatred of the Other!

All of this go totally against the Dhamma and is an unpardonable insult to the Buddha. This I say not to wear my belief in the Dhamma on my sleeve, but to explain to my fellow multi-religious Sri Lankans and others who may be thoroughly flummoxed by the current goings-on in this country in the name of Buddhism. If culture-worshipping Sinhala-Buddhists get offended by it, hard luck!

As a citizen of the Democratic Socialist Republic of Sri Lanka and as per the supreme law of this land, its Constitution Chapter III (Article14), I too have the freedom and right of speech, expression as well as publication. Hence in this book, I have exercised my rights accordingly.

Over the years, I have been forced to suffer the tight-assed versions of hypocritical Cultural Sinhala-Buddhism. I dumped those I could and endured the rest! Some such Cultural Sinhala-Buddhists claim I have 'attacked' Buddhism through some of my published pieces in the past. If what they refer to as 'Buddhism' is the 'culture' they venerate as opposed to the philosophy, then, most definitely, "yes". I have indeed attacked such. But if I stand accused of attacking the Philosophical Dhamma, they couldn't be more wrong!

Then came the Rajapaksa regime and this anathematic term 'Sinhala-Buddhist' raised its ugly head again and was donned like a crown of glory by Rajapaksa himself. One not very fine day, towards my final days at SCOPP, I received a phone call from the Presidential Secretariat. The caller wanted me to compere/host an event where the Head of State, Mahinda Rajapaksa, would preside. Since the request was informal and outside the functions of my role and responsibilities as Director Communications of SCOPP, I refused despite SCOPP coming directly under the purview of the President. I suggested instead the name of a broadcaster colleague of mine to the caller. His immediate response was, "He's not a Sinhala-Buddhist. We want a Sinhala-Buddhist"!

On the verge of rupturing a blood vessel, I slammed the receiver down. This is when it dawned on me where the country was heading under the Rajapaksa regime!

As a Sinhalese and a follower of the Philosophical Dhamma domiciled in Sri Lanka, I feel utterly helpless, hopeless, guilty, embarrassed, ashamed and sorry for what has been done and continues to be done by a handful of maniacal 'Sinhala-Buddhist' bigots against my fellow Sri Lankans of minority ethnic and religious groups. And the silence in the face of such injustice by others like myself was and is pathetically deafening!

Some of the chapters contained in this book are similar in essence to my articles published a few years back. However, upon revisiting them, I realised that I sounded like a hysterical child screaming in anger and frustration. Hence, I have rewritten them entirely, introducing a semblance of sanity and hopefully common sense.

Also, as a Philosophical Buddhist, I have intentionally avoided writing on the conclusion of the civil war in 2009, though I have referred to it in passing in these pages. In this book, I have strived to follow George Eliot's advice, "The finest language is mostly made up of simple unimposing words". I hope I have done the lady justice.

Last but not least, my heartfelt gratitude to my dear friends John and Daleena for their invaluable assistance in editing this book.

- Sharmini Dias Nagahawatte Serasinghe

Return of the Tyrant

On 19 November 2005, Percy Mahendra (Mahinda) Rajapaksa assumed the mantle of the sixth Executive President of Sri Lanka. Many of us, including diehard UNP supporters, hailed him as a true son of the soil who would finally make things right for our tattered nation. Such was the hope we optimists had in him.

Some even paid him backhanded compliments such as, "Mahinda is one president who has blundered his way to success". At the time it sounded funny, but true. After all, he was the pleasant and simple village guy, forever the underdog in the political arena, who catapulted to the top and had to grope his way around. But he appeared to be getting it right eventually, though rather clumsily.

He did what all of his predecessor didn't have it in them to do; grant carte blanche to the three-Armed Forces to rid the country of LTTE tyranny, once and for all. For this, the masses bowed to him with gratitude and relief. Hence, he shall go down in history as the leader who set us free from a ruthless terrorist outfit!

But, then, one of man's greatest failings – greed coupled with ego – got the better of him. Consumed by 'We Won the War' mania, his sole qualification to ensure a second term in office, he began his descent. When the masses, hypnotized by his 'We Won the War' mantra, voted him in with their hearts and not their heads for a second term in 2010, he lost it even further. His over-inflated ego became the Executive President of Sri Lanka and, thus, he lost touch with reality!

Had he the grace to retire with dignity and pass the baton on to another, he would well have gone down in Sri Lanka's recent history as one of the greatest heroes this country has ever known. But, no, he was insatiable! Sycophants around him helped him dig deeper into his own political grave by buttressing his already massive ego by labelling him the 'Uncrowned King of Sri Lanka'. Thus, he became Sri Lanka's 'Emperor in New Clothes'.

Rajapaksa appeared to believe that he had every right to rule Sri Lanka ad infinitum as an uncrowned king. What he subsequently did to ensure that is now old hat.

As Maithripala Sirisena stated in his address to the nation as Sri Lanka's seventh President, "This country needs an ordinary man to serve its people, as its 'Chief Servant', NOT a King!"

Rajapaksa's first faux pas amongst many was the bull-in-a-china-shop manner in which he dealt with his predecessor Chandrika Bandaranaike Kumaratunga. Had he heeded his common sense and not his injured ego, he might have known better than to mess with the lady. Kumaranatunge returned for vengeance, buried the hatchet with her former bête noire, Ranil Wickremesinghe, and gave Rajapaksa the works. And she still appears to be doing it from behind the scenes.

Next on his ever-growing list of faux pas was the appointment of a humongous Cabinet of Ministers, Deputies and Whatnots; a Guinness World Record, to secure his position. It comprised the likes of Mervyn Silva, unfit, even to sweep the floors of the hallowed Parliament. Even a zoo-keeper might have found it challenging to control such a depraved mob. I'm sure even Rajapaksa himself didn't know who most of his Ministers, Deputies and MPs were; there were so many in the circus he called a Cabinet.

Then he went the unforgivable step further by stoking the tinderbox of ethno-religious extremism. He turned a blind eye to 'Buddhist' extremists such as Galagoda Aththe Gnanasara and his Bodu Bala Sena (BBS), the Sinhala Ravaya (SR), the Ravana Balaya (RB) and such others, while they went on the rampage against the Other. Only a morally-bankrupt demagogue would resort to using ethno-religious extremism to hold on to power the way Rajapaksa did.

No matter what these saffron-robed goons did to insult and harm our fellow Sri Lankans of the Muslim and Christian faiths,

Rajapaksa appeared to simply look the other way. By doing so, he made the already farcical identity of this nation's image as a 'Buddhist country' a hilarious mockery.

And despite all this, Mahinda Rajapaksa calls himself a practicing Buddhist. If so, where was *metta*, loving kindness; *karuna*, compassion; *mudita*, sympathetic joy; and *upekkha*, equanimity, in his definition of Buddhism towards the minorities? Was he and is he still hoping to be the demagogic leader of only the Sinhala-Buddhists of Sri Lanka?

Never did we Sri Lankans   the Sinhalese, Tamils and Muslims feel so polarized on the grounds of our ethnicity and religious beliefs as under the Rajapaksa leadership. For this, he ought to hang his head in shame! Had 51.3 percent of our people not stood their ground on 8 January 2015, we would have been looking at another protracted war, this time on ethno-religious grounds of mind-boggling proportions.

Furthermore, those very same demons he was pampering might have ended up strangling him with his own *kurakkan sathakaya*. Remember what became of President Premadasa after pandering to the enemy by gifting arms and weapons to the LTTE? Remember what Somarama did to Prime Minister S. W. R. D. Bandaranaike?

Any leader who remains too long at the helm, like Rajapaksa did, loses touch with reality. The common man he wooed with false hopes and promises to vote for him was forgotten and left to rot. The 'good life' at the top and all the pampered glory that went with it gave him amnesia. Come the next election and we shall see the whole drama reenacted. What blatant hypocrisy!

Then there was that abominable 'Victory Day' in the month of May, which Rajapaksa insisted on 'celebrating', come hell or high water. The vulgar display of pomp and pageantry in the most crass and tasteless way possible associated with this event made many of us sick to our stomachs. The LTTE was a home-grown terrorist outfit and not a foreign invader. All those who lost their lives or became destitute because of a civil war rooted by Rajapaksa's own political predecessors were/are also our very own countrymen, women and children; Sri Lankans are of all ethnic groups and include Tamils. So, what in heaven's name was this 'Victory Day' celebrated for, except to buttress Rajapaksa's already overinflated ego!

Consumed by the 'We Won the War' mania, Rajapaksa totally ignored the God-given opportunity to finally do right by the Tamil community of this country. Totally self-absorbed, the man's vision and direction were instead focused on becoming 'King of Sinhala-Buddhist Sri Lanka'. He even went to the extent of imposing a de facto ban on Sri Lanka's national anthem being sung in Tamil.

Little did he care how this would translate into a serious obstacle to post-conflict reconciliation. Or was that the intention?

Apparently not satisfied with keeping the Sinhalese and Tamils polarized, he next went on to divide the Sinhalese and Muslims as well by allowing the likes of the maniacal and racist Sinhala-Buddhist BBS with Gnanasara at the helm to run amok. What on earth was he hoping to achieve by fanning and keeping alive the embers of discord among the populace?

The humiliation of defeat when he was eyeing a third term as President must undoubtedly have been tough for one such as Rajapaksa. The transition from 'Honourable' to 'nothing' must surely have been unbearable.

Is war, death and destruction so profitable for the few? Will such a man ever regret all the wrongs he allowed to happen under his very nose? Do humans like Mahinda Rajapaksa have a conscience?

Satan Dons the Saffron Robe

"A tyrant must put on the appearance of uncommon devotion to religion. Subjects are less apprehensive of illegal treatment from a ruler whom they consider god-fearing and pious. On the other hand, they do less easily move against him, believing that he has the gods on his side."   Aristotle

Aristotle might have envisioned the likes of Mahinda Rajapaksa of Sri Lanka with despotic tendencies when he uttered these wise words. Sri Lankans have short memories. That's a time-tested fact especially when it comes to the ballot. Well into his second term in office, the luster of Rajapaksa's 'We Won the War' mantra was

fading fast, and he knew it. Every form of ineptitude corruption, nepotism, cronyism, abuse of power, and scandals, coupled with a bull-in-the-china-shop style of governance and foreign policy   became the norm from top down and was rapidly

becoming synonymous with his regime. Obvious attempts to remain at the helm of political power *ad infinitum* had started to grate on many a nerve.

Hence, while in his second term in office, the man consumed by greed started eyeing a third term. With Rajapaksa's now politically-bankrupt leadership, and with his sole qualification to remain in power being his war victory, he needed to justify his continuance to the gullible voter by producing yet another 'monster' threatening the peace and stability of the country. Rajapaksa marketed himself as the only leader Sri Lanka will ever know who can protect the insecure amongst the majority Sinhala-Buddhists from any monster, namely the LTTE, by humming his mantra "We won the War!" *ad nauseam,* and thus hypnotising and convincing the gullible amongst the populace.

The politically time-tested trick in the bag that has thus far yielded excellent results since independence is Sinhala-Buddhist nationalism, including the much used and abused yet all-powerful saffron robe. Politicians of yore discovered it and their successors, perhaps with the exception of J. R. Jayawardena, never let go of it, making it almost a tradition in the local political spectrum. The power it wields knows no bounds, as the intellectually-handicapped amongst the voters are ever willing to fall flat on their faces and worship anything or anyone draped in a saffron robe. It's almost a reflex action entrenched in their psyche. Thus, they can be hoodwinked into believing, doing or turning a blind eye to almost anything, as long as it is said and done by one clad in a saffron robe.

The saffron robe symbolises all that the Buddha stood for. However, He never intended for it to be worshipped and revered. This sacred robe was thus turned into both shield and weapon against the very teachings of the Buddha. For those sincere and genuine amongst our Buddhist clergy, this amounts to downright sacrilege. As for those marauding charlatans impersonating Buddhist monks, to hell with the *Vinaya Pitaka* (the code of conduct for Buddhist monks, one of the three books that make up the *Tripitaka*); the saffron robe became a conveniently powerful strategy to wreak havoc with impunity. These pseudo-monks have become a sheer disgrace to the Buddha, the Dhamma and its true followers. For the demagogue Rajapaksa, these saffron-robed ruffians seemed to be his ultimate 'power tool' for perpetual control of political power.

The Grease Yakka Phenomenon

I have often wondered if there ever was a connection between the infamous 'Grease Yakkas' who emerged in 2011, their subsequent disappearance, and the emergence of the belligerent monks of the Bodu Bala Sena (BBS) in 2012/13. Who on earth were these Grease Yakkas? Are they the same characters who shaved their heads and donned saffron robes later? The Grease Yakkas operated mainly in rural parts of the Muslim and Tamil-majority areas in the northern and central parts of the island and attacked mostly Tamil and Muslim women. Reportedly, there was a stark lack of any serious attempts by the Rajapaksa regime to investigate and apprehend these miscreants.

The obvious inaction by law enforcement and Government agencies under the Rajapaksa regime in this regard painted a bigger and uglier picture. The systemic failure of the rule of law in the North and East and the blatant unwillingness of the Rajapaksa regime to hold the assailants accountable strongly alluded to who was behind the whole disgusting drama. But, why? Was it an attempt to keep the minorities forever on edge and in fear for their lives? The Women's Action Network (WAN), an umbrella organization made up of eight women's organizations working actively in the North and East, stated in its preliminary report the various acts of omission and commission by state agencies, defence officials, media and vigilante groups regarding this matter.

According to WAN, in August 2011, many women in the North and the East had been attacked individually, and the female population in general, terrorised by these Grease Yakkas. Women in the war-torn North and East in particular were and are a vulnerable lot. Most had lost their fathers, brothers, husbands and sons to a protracted civil war they never asked for. Post war, they were already burdened by the responsibilities of heading their households single-handedly and rebuilding a life for themselves and their families when the Grease Yakkas struck. What kind of man and leader was Rajapaksa to ignore such cowardly attacks against women? Doesn't he himself have a mother, sisters and a wife?

Hot on the heels of the monstrous 'Grease Yakkas', who disappeared as fast as they appeared, out popped from nowhere, a gang of saffron-robed renegades. They were/are supposed to be Buddhist monks, but their behaviour and disposition were more akin to a state-sponsored paramilitary outfit with an agenda. This time around, they chose their garb ingeniously. Instead of grease-smeared bodies and faces painted black, they donned the sacred saffron robe which granted them carte blanch to behave in any which way they wished, with the long arm of the law looking the other way. Meanwhile, the demagogues feigned innocence and overtly sermonised the merits of ethno-religious harmony and other such politically-correct platitudes. At the same time, they appeared to be giving covert succor to the saffron-robed renegades by allowing them to run amok with impunity, reducing the law enforcement authorities to a state of *reductio ad absurdum*.

The uninformed voter has difficulty discerning the difference between these 'monks' and the average *Swaminwahanse* from their village temple. They are unable to see beyond the saffron robe and realise that they are nothing but a group of extremist bigots, hell-bent on wreaking havoc and destroying any semblance of peace post-war, finally emerging in this tattered land.

Few realise that most Buddhist monks of today don't take up robes to spread the message of the Dhamma. I bet my bottom dollar they don't even understand it. Some are forced into monkhood as young children by their parents to enjoy the benefits of the education system accorded to Buddhist monks and other reasons I have explained later in this book. Yet others are nothing but lazy freeloaders who don the saffron robe to live a life of *dolce far niente* for the rest of their days. The minds of such 'monks' with interest in anything but the Dhamma are the playground of the Devil's workshop. It is most disturbing to see today even young 'Samaneras' or novice monks being made to contribute to hate speech and vile demonstrations against the Other. Far too many of these impressionable young children have been offered, gifted, abandoned or donated to the 'temple' and ought to be in school. Instead they roam the streets with their older counterparts watching, learning and emulating the evil ways of their mentors.

Now that these 'monks' have been unleashed with apparent political blessings, the demagogues will soon find themselves caught between the devil and the deep blue sea. There may soon come a day when these 'monks' and their lay supporters will no longer be satisfied to just dance to the tunes of their masters but seek a greater political role. That would be the day Sri Lanka turns into a Sinhala-Buddhist Saudi Arabia. With the obvious immunity enjoyed by the saffron-robed, we now see every Tom, Dick and Harry starting to masquerade as Buddhist monks. Who is empowered to check their bona fides? Left unchecked, these yellow-robed renegades will eventually 'take over' the country as they are 'in it' for the bigger and longer haul. It is just a matter of time before this saga blows up in the very faces of those who fanned its flames   the Rajapaksas.

Hypothetically, what if they decide to go on a rampage of a much larger scale than we have witnessed so far? What if the armed forces are called upon to subdue them; how would they possibly distinguish a genuine Buddhist monk from an imposter? Would they be called upon to turn their guns on the entire Buddhist clergy of this country? Would they be tarred with the same brush, in the way all Tamils were perceived as terrorists and all Muslims as Jihadists?

We as a nation have collectively suffered a thirty-year war, seasoned with JVP insurrections in between. Hence, the last thing we need is an ethno-religious war which would undoubtedly be of much greater and inconceivable proportions. Politicians like hurricanes come and go; it is the destruction they leave behind that we Lankans and our future generations are stuck with.

Stirring the Pot of Religious Extremism

With the end of the almost thirty-year civil war in 2009, the dawn
of 2013 saw the rise of a new potential terrorist threat: saffron-clad
groups calling themselves Bodu Bala Senawa (BBS), Sinhala
Ravaya (SR) and Ravana Balaya (RB). They crawled out of the
woodwork waving the flag of Sinhala-Buddhist supremacism,
nationalism, extremism, racism   call it what you may   in the
face of the other. Their saffron camouflage was the perfect
disguise for the havoc they wrought with impunity. For the average
undiscriminating culture-customs-traditions-worshipping Buddhist
lacking true inner sight into the Dhamma, even a saffron robe-
wrapped broomstick is worthy of falling flat on their faces and
worshipping. Hence, these new Sinhala-Buddhist overbearing
bigots faced little resistance to their goal to establish Sri Lanka as a
'Sinhala-Buddhist Dictatorship'.

Never in our recent history have we seen anything similar to the
Rajapaksa culture of racist Sinhala-Buddhist supremacism and
attempts to establish a 'Sinhala-Buddhist Autocracy' in Sri Lanka.
It was a 'new' for this country and was born during the regime of
none other than the 'Good Buddhist' Mahinda Rajapaksa himself,

who seemingly gave the groups *carte blanche* to run amok. Instead of nipping this sociological scourge that surfaced during his regime in the bud, Rajapaksa appeared to give succor to it by turning a blind eye. The endgame of these groups appeared to be to juxtapose the majority Buddhists and the minority communities of the country and classify the latter as inferior. This caused and continues to cause irreparable damage to the process of peace and reconciliation in post-war Sri Lanka. The well-orchestrated Aluthgama riots against Muslims in June 2014 and those in Ampara and Kandy in 2018 bore all the hallmarks of these 'religious' extremists and were classic cases in point. It was almost *déjà vu* of those dark days of the July 1983 riots targetting Tamils. In both instances, the law enforcement authorities failed to act on the carnage that took place under their very noses before it got out of control. With the change of political regimes in January 2015, many of us heaved a sigh of relief for different reasons. The minorities, I'm sure, did so hoping for a final peace under a more inclusive administration. But the malignant roots of the cancer of religious extremism which Rajapaksa stoked continued to spread and will do so if he returns to the helm by fair means or foul.

For a while it seemed the saffron-robed brigades had been reined in and silenced, with the regime change in 2015. But then along came a new player into the game in 2016, a clone of Gnanasara and his BBS: Yakkalamulle Pawara and his Sinhale Jathika

Balamuluwa, claiming to 'safeguard the identity of the Sinhala people and to regenerate the supremacy and pride of the Sinhala people'. Good grief! Do these people honestly believe the Sinhalese are vulnerable to losing their identity and need safeguarding? Nevertheless, in this context, the lower-middle class Sinhala-Buddhist is a vulnerable customer in the marketplace of such supremacist politics. This underprivileged class is, alas, in the majority. They are also gullible and lack common sense. Their daily struggle to make ends meet make them blind to the bigger picture and are easily convinced of the veracity of the dubious patriotism and supremist fantasies that the saffron-robed, the likes of Mahinda Rajapaksa and his cohorts' fan in their faces.

To excite these gullible groups, they spin fantastic tales from the Mahavamsa about the superiority of a 2,500-year-old culture, the remnants of which stand today only as archeological ruins and edifices, much like the morals of most of the heirs to this 'culture' who uphold these monuments as iconic achievements of the ultimate human race   the Sinhala-Buddhists. How this 'supreme race' has failed in recent times to live up to this lofty 'culture' is mindboggling.

Hosannas on Sri Lanka's 2,500-year old culture have been one man's meat and another man's poison since independence. Whenever a Sinhalese with an inferiority complex coupled with a racist mindset finds himself stumped, the much-hackneyed theme of a 2,500-year old culture and the achievements of our great kings of ancient times are brought to play. But no reference is made to what the Sinhalese have achieved and contributed to perpetuate this grandiose culture since independence. Why? Because we the Sinhalese have done nothing for our country to speak of, except drag it down into the dumps! While our ancestors didn't need foreign aid and assistance to build what they did, their pathetic descendants of today are unable to construct even a road without crying out for foreign help.

I recall, as an impressionable teenager, the first state visit to the USA by Sri Lanka's first Executive President, J. R. Jayawardene, during Ronald Reagan's tenure as President. In his televised address on the South Lawn of the White House, Jayawardene, casting aside his *noblesse oblige*, referred to the United States as "a country with 'only' a 200-year-old history, while Sri Lanka's was over 2,500 years old". This casual or calculated remark (with JRJ one never knew) has remained with me to date. At the time, I couldn't help but feel that it reeked of an acute inferiority complex, and I was utterly embarrassed on his behalf.

For most of us Sri Lankans who have heard this tosh too often, it holds no water. But to a foreigner hearing of 'Sri Lanka's 2,500-year old culture' and seeing for themselves how this 'great' culture has shaped this country's fortunes and misfortunes, it must be truly overwhelming. Within such a context they must also see that the citizenry of this 'Buddhist country' comprise not only Sinhalese and Buddhists but Tamils, Muslims, Burghers, Hindus, Christians, Moslems and others who also have every right to call this country their motherland. They too are a significant part of the rich cultural and historical fabric of this country – a fact that many racist Sinhala-Buddhists prefer not to acknowledge, and instead regard and treat them as the 'Other', 'Occupants' or 'Guests' of this 'Sinhala-Buddhist country'. These Sinhala-Buddhists sincerely believe that Sri Lanka is a Buddhist country because they have been brainwashed for aeons into believing that the Buddha himself chose this land over and above all others to foster and perpetuate his Dhamma. Had the wise Buddha done so, which I seriously doubt, he made an unpardonable *faux pas*.

To those outsiders who know and understand the Theravada teachings of the Buddha, it must indeed be strange to see how the Buddhists of this 'Buddhist country' with an ancient cultural heritage actually practice the Teachings, starting with its so-called guardians, the caste-conscious Mahanayakes. They must notice that most amongst the Buddhist monks, Bhikkus, the living symbols of this ancient culture, are not quite abiding by the rules of the Vinaya Pitaka, the code of conduct for Buddhist monks. For instance, the repugnant caste system, denounced by the Buddha himself, is practised and fostered amongst the prominent Buddhist clergy in this 'Buddhist country' through caste-based '*nikayas*'. Some of these Bhikkus lead materialistic lives, travelling and living in luxury, engaging in business and finance and even owning property, while the Buddhist laity including politicians of successive governments, spin on their heads venerating them like gods.

In addition, one would expect tolerance and compassion to reign supreme in a 'Buddhist country' which holds such rich claims to the Buddha and his Teachings. But no! Perhaps the moral lows we have sunk to as a people would not be so stark if the trumpets of its glorious past are not blown so loud. Talk about empty vessels making the most noise!

The Tragicomic 'Sinha-Le' Tribe

It is indeed ironic and tragically hilarious that while our Sinhala-Buddhists boast of a 2,500-year-old culture and one of the highest literacy rates in Asia, there are those today claiming a bloodline to a four-legged beast, the lion! The apparently delusional 'Sinha-Le' (Lion-blood) tribe is unable to differentiate allegory and myth as per the *Mahavamsa* from fact. After all, the ability to read and write defined as 'high literacy' in Sri Lanka doesn't guarantee intelligence, common sense or wisdom, does it?

What is most hilarious is that by claiming ancestry to a beast, they are also inadvertently admitting to being sub-human   qualities they have no qualms about displaying unashamedly in the public arena. Is this what our 2,500-year-old culture has produced?

This unique beast-blooded tribe, which also appears to have inherited its level of intelligence and lethargy, seems unable to distinguish between the Dhamma and the Mahawamsa. Yet they insist on calling themselves 'Buddhists' and 'guardians of Buddhism'. The lion that gave rise to this progeny must surely hang its head in shame, while those of us Sinhalese fortunate to have human blood running though our veins instead of that of a beast can only shake our heads in despair!

Typical to the nature of this part-beast tribe, gullibility is also in their genes. Hence, it is no surprise at all they have yet again fallen, hook, line and sinker for a desperate and devious effort by those who bit the dust in the January 2015 General Elections. 'Sinha Le' is their latest tragicomedy. Unsurprisingly once again, it is the lion-blooded saffron-robed who are its main actors, performing at their best. When, oh when, will these fallen despots cease to use the saffron-robed as a means to their dubious ends?

While all human-blooded Buddhists agree that the Dhamma needs no protection from any force, constitution or human, the image of Sri Lanka as a Buddhist country has suffered immensely, not at the hands of Others but at the paws of the subhuman Sinha Le-Buddhists who have become a tribe unto themselves! In the name of national interest, why do we need Buddhist monks to stir the pot of politics when we have an abundance of the laity in parliament to do the needful?

For centuries past, the sangha merely played the role of advisors to the rulers of this country, as opposed to actively engaging in politics. They didn't meddle in matters of governance and become a nuisance to the public as is the norm today. Hence their active interference in national interests thus far has only been to the nation's detriment; making the process of peace and reconciliation a near impossibility in this land!

National interest is the business of the multi-ethnic laity of Sri Lanka and not of Buddhist monks, who are supposed to have renounced all and broken the fetters that tie them to lay life to follow the path of the Dhamma. Those who insist on taking up worldly life must disrobe before doing so. This is ethically the right thing to do as per the Vinaya Pitaka. However, as the Sinhe-Le cannot wield power without the saffron robe, they have a need to eat the cake and have it too!

The moral depths the Sinha-Le tribe has sunk to is an indictment of how these messengers of the Buddha's teachings (Buddhist monks) have failed in their mission thus far. Instead of interfering in matters of national political affairs, the Sangha needs to return to their true calling and practice as well as propagate the message of the Learned One, the Buddha.

Sri Lanka's post-independence political history is replete with how the interference of Buddhist monks in issues of national interest have been to the detriment of this land. Is this to be the tradition continued? How much longer are we to put up with it?

The Demagogic Rajapaksa Wants a Comeback

The dawn of 2015 gave many of us Sri Lankans fresh hope. The megalomaniac and demagogic Rajapaksa and his bandwagon were finally out. Many of us voted for Maithripala Sirisena not knowing who or what he was simply to be rid of the tyrannical Mahinda Rajapaksa. We might even have voted for a buffalo for that matter. Such was our desperation to be rid of the man. But, we were looking to the statesman Prime Minster Ranil Wickremesinghe to put the country back on track. Regrettably, from a sociopolitical perspective, we are still trying to emerge from the mess created by Rajapaksa. Once again, we are being subjected to yet another ludicrous comedy of errors unfolding on the political stage of Sri Lanka.

Since independence, this stage has witnessed many such performances enacted by 'comedians' of all political hues. The current farce takes the cake. 'Good Governance' aka 'Yahapalana' was fanciful right from the start. In a country where rouges, thugs, drug lords, rapists, child molesters, murders et al call the shots, and are seemingly above the law, with some of their puppets masquerading as politicians, how on earth can there be good governance?

Civil society, the multi-religious clergy, the media and a handful of honest citizens have been shouting themselves hoarse, calling to rid the stage of these political dregs. While this is indeed long overdue, given the quality of 'politicians' we are left to choose from, and with 'Messrs. Honest/Clean Citizen' in society refusing to get their hands dirty in the stinking mire of politics, what choice do we have?

We have a former president, a one-time hero who is today perceived as a villain by many, who cooked his goose on 8 January 2015. He is now hell-bent on making a comeback by fair means or foul, with his bull-in-a-china-shop antics, to do what he knows best; drive the country further down the hole he started digging between 2009 and 2015. Has this man no scruples!

And we have his successor who stabbed his predecessor in the back and vowed in his address to the nation in January 2015 to remain in office only until the end of his first term. However, he did the expected *volte-face* and is now caught between the devil and the deep blue sea; he has cooked his own goose even before his first term ended. The man has proved to be a double-crossing traitor who singlehandedly made a mockery of our Constitution and kicked us   the citizens of Sri Lanka   in our faces. For this,

President Maithripala Sirisena ought to be impeached, stripped of his civil rights and tried for treason.

When J.R. Jayawardene introduced the Executive Presidential system, he argued that a strong Executive President would hold the country together whenever the stability of Parliament and the country were threatened. He obviously did not envision such powers falling into the hands of the likes of Maithripala Sirisena who singlehandedly did the exact opposite   destabilised Parliament and the entire country   for which we the citizens of Sri Lanka will be called upon to pay the ultimate price.

Allegations of human rights violations, corruption ranging from abuse of power, to attacks on the media, abduction and killing of journalists, plunder and waste of public wealth, fraud and election malpractices by the Rajapaksas have yet to be proven in a court of law. This has now paved the way for a Rajapaksa comeback, hopefully, *pro tem*.

Further, there are many myopic halfwits out there who are still awestruck by 'nice roads, pavements, parks, and buildings etc.' built during the Rajapaksa era. They seem to believe they were built with the private funds of the Rajapaksas. Fortunately, this group is but a minuscule and insignificant minority, comprising mainly socialites of Colombo who frequent the cocktail circuit and who believe it's beneath their dignity to stand in a queue and rub shoulders with the common man to cast their vote. So, they don't vote! Come what may, they are a happy lot as long as they are surrounded by a pleasant veneer.

And then there are those still on reverse gear, waving the 'They Won the War' flag! Haven't 'they', servants of the public living off the tax payer, been appreciated and thanked enough?

To the objective and detached, these are indeed interesting times!

Gotabbels to Turn Gotler?

"If you tell a lie big enough and keep repeating it, people will eventually come to believe it. The lie can be maintained only for such time as the State can shield the people from the political, economic and/or military consequences of the lie. It thus becomes vitally important for the State to use all of its powers to repress dissent, for the truth is the mortal enemy of the lie, and thus by extension, the truth is the greatest enemy of the State."   Joseph Goebbels.

This statement, made over seventy years ago by the Nazi Paul Joseph Goebbels of the Third Reich, has some parallels to what went on in Sri Lanka during the Rajapaksa regime. We had Goebbels reincarnated under our very noses!

To avoid confusion between the late German Nazi and his living local counterpart, let me call him Gotabbels. Further, while there are many similarities between the two, our man is not cast in the exact same mold as his German version, who was the Minister for Public Enlightenment and Propaganda of Nazi Germany.

Goebbels was one of German dictator Adolf Hitler's closest associates and most devout followers. Our Gotabbels is, or should it now be 'was', also the closest associate and most devout follower of his sibling, who we shall call Mahabbels.

While Goebbels earned a Ph.D., his 'clone' of Sinhala-Buddhist descent didn't. An early and avid supporter of war, Goebbels did everything in his power to prepare the German people for a large-scale military conflict, just like our Gotabbels did. However, our man eventually put an end to a scourge   kudos to him for that! Yes, the tax-payer paid for his salary and perks, but he well deserved them because he delivered the goods expected of him.

Goebbels intensified the propaganda machine by urging the Germans to accept the idea of total war. But our man ran into some trouble in this area initially because our independent media had a mind of its own. However, Gotabbels overcame that opposition by any means – fair or foul.

Goebbels had a sharp tongue which made him enemies within the Nazi Party. Our man has one too, which earned him enemies amongst the private media but not within the party he supported. Or that's what seemed to be on the surface. The state-owned media of course was not a problem because bootlickers were appointed to head them who did the usual "Yes sir, yes sir, three bags full sir" number, which was expected of them.

Goebbels knew the power of controlling the people's minds; our man thought he could do that too, but didn't quite succeed, except for the gullible and brainwashed Sinhala-Buddhists.

With Goebbels, those who did not toe the line had to face the Gestapo, the Secret Police. With our Gotabbels, well, let's not go there because those who are in the know, know!

A tireless, tenacious agitator with the gift of paralysing opponents by a guileful combination of venom, slander and insinuation, Goebbels knew how to mobilize the fears of the masses. Our Gotabbels too had mastered that art to perfection, especially with and through our media.

Goebbels became editor of *Das Reich*, writing regular front-page 'editorials' and lauding the successes of the German forces. Gotabbel's sycophants did something similar by operating a website on similar lines, which we journalists were very familiar with. It carried a lot of Gotabbels's propaganda, in addition to attacking certain journalists who stubbornly refused to keep their traps shut.

Goebbels advocated progressively harsher discrimination, including the extermination of the Jews in the Holocaust. Now, doesn't that ring a bell regarding our Gotabbels and his Sinhala-Buddhist bandwagon?

Goebbels personally supervised the deportation of Jews from Berlin and proposed that Jews along with Gypsies be regarded as 'unconditionally exterminable'.

On 7 June 2007, here in Sri Lanka, several hundreds of Northern and Eastern Tamils residing in lodges in Colombo were forcibly evicted from their homes and packed off to whereever they came from, in what was termed as part of a 'security-related measure'. Fortunately, the Supreme Court ruled against this despicable move, and two days later these 'expelled' citizens of Sri Lanka were returned to Colombo.

In the evening of 30 April 1945, with the Soviet troops just a few hundred yards away, Adolf Hitler killed himself. In accordance with his will, Goebbels succeeded him as Chancellor of Germany. However, he served just one day in this post. The following day, 1 May 1945, Goebbels and his wife committed suicide, after poisoning their six children with cyanide.

No, we do not wish this fate upon our Gotabbels and his family!

And now, there are very ominous sounds to the tune of Gotabbels's plans to become Gotler of Sri Lanka. Good grief!!!

Having always advocated a benevolent/democratic dictator for Sri Lanka similar to Lee Kuan Yew of Singapore and Mahathir Mohamad of Malaysia, Gotler would have been the perfect choice but for his militaristic and nationalistic/racist Sinhala-Buddhist mindset that makes him a definite no-no!

Gotabbels is an ex-military officer and if we have the misfortune of having him as our next President, moderate Buddhist Sinhalese and all the rest, except of course for the racist Sinhala-Buddhists, will have no option but to flee our land of birth or remain as docile and subjugated subjects.

Alarmingly, those who are reportedly aiding and abetting the 'Gotler' project are said to be a group of military officers obviously with a war-mongering mindset. If their project comes to pass, Sri Lanka will end up with an extreme version of Sinhalese-Buddhist nationalism and militarism; a Sinhala-Buddhist Saudi Arabia. Our country will cease to uphold any tenets of modern democracy, including freedom of speech and expression, human rights, minority rights, constitutionalism, and accountability. In short, all constraints imposed by democratic norms and practices will in all probability cease.

A highly-centralised military system of governance with Gotler at the helm, free of all the shackles of democratic norms and practices, seems to be what we will have to live with ad infinitum for when the likes of Gotler occupy the top seat, they never leave! Many Sinhala-Buddhists, including wealthy saffron-robed landlords, businessmen who got rich virtually overnight during the demagogic regime of the past, reportedly regard direct involvement in the political administration of the country as an investment for personal wealth enhancement. They are among those who want to see Sri Lanka Gotlerised!

Absit omen!

The Dhamma needs no Protection from the Constitution

For what purpose and for whose benefit is Article 9 of Chapter II of the Constitution of Sri Lanka, which specifically states "The Republic of Sri Lanka shall give to Buddhism the foremost place and accordingly it shall be the duty of the State to protect and foster the Buddha Sasana?"

For well over 2,500 years, the Buddha Dhamma has survived without any constitutional 'protection' and will continue to do so amongst those who understand and practice it for as long as mankind exists.

To Philosophical Buddhist, the Dhamma will always occupy the foremost place in our hearts and minds and needs no protection from anything or anyone, least of all a mere mention on paper, the Constitution, ensuring its supreme status.

But not so for the hypocritical saffron-robed and lay Cultural Buddhists of Sri Lanka who are making a hue and cry for the inclusion of the unamended Article 9 in Chapter II of the proposed new Constitution. It is obvious that it is they who want State assurance in continuing to protect, foster and give pride of place to their Sinhala-Buddhism and the Sinhala-Buddhist establishment which they call the 'Buddha Sasana', thus relegating other religions and faiths to underdog status.

All things fake have weak foundations and never last!

If Sinhala-Buddhism is to continue, its guardians, the saffron-robed Cultural Sinhala-Buddhists, will definitely need the protection of the State and the Constitution. The nonsensical 'religion' behind which they seek refuge is founded on nothing but lies, deceit, bigotry and hypocrisy; the very antithesis of the Dhamma. Hence, they need to be propped up by Constitutions and governments in power.

As I have mentioned many a time before, the only claim these men in robes have to monkhood is the saffron robe they wear. Once disrobed, they lose their power, status and reverence.

It is incumbent upon the State to repair the damage done to the image of Buddhism in this country by none other than these so-called Buddhist monks. They should be banned across the board from engaging in politics and other business of the laity. If they must, then they ought to be ordered to disrobe, and punished for desecrating the image of Buddhism in this country and the saffron robe they hide beneath. These charlatans masquerading as Buddhist monks have used and abused the sacred saffron robe associated with the Buddha for too long. It's time to call a halt!

Politics is the business of the laity and concerns only the laity, not Buddhist monks. Hence, they should be ordered to keep their opinions relating to political matters of the laity to themselves, unless asked for.

Instead of religion, what the Constitution needs to protect, foster and prioritise is unity, peace and reconciliation in a secular Sri Lanka. Despite the near three-decade-old-civil war having ended almost a decade ago, we are still a very long way from healing, reconciliation and national integration. Notably, if we are to avoid yet another civil war in the future, giving the foremost place to Buddhism in our Constitution is not the answer. In fact, it would be to its detriment and will only precipitate it, as it was this very clause in the previous and existing Constitutions that contributed to the Tamil Separatist uprising in the first instance.

Societies that fail to learn from past mistakes, fail to build sustainable peace. This country has suffered one conflict after another, both in the North and South, because government after government ignored the past and failed to learn from mistakes made. Hence the entire country suffered, not just the Sinhalese and Tamils, but all of us!

Ten years post-war and the memories of the horrors we endured are still fresh in our minds. Such memories don't go away easily especially when grievances are left unaddressed and ignored. If not addressed now, these grievances can continue forever like a genetic birth-defect, passing down the generations and become entrenched in our psyche. This will undoubtedly carry the risk of a ceaseless cycle of violence in the future.

Is that the legacy we will be leaving for the future generations of Sri Lanka?

Mahavamsaism   The Scourge of Lanka

Few of my tribe would agree that the *Mahavamsa* has been more to the detriment than to the good of Sri Lanka. Intentionally or not, many 'nationalists' have failed or refused to understand that its contents are nothing more an "epic poem for the serene joy and emotion of the pious", interlacing legends and myths about the history of this country. They cloud the present with the mythical past chronicled in its pages that supports Sinhala-Buddhist nationalism, thus transforming it into the 'sacred scourge of Sri Lanka'. At a time when Buddhism began to lose its popularity in India, the monks of the Mahavihara designated this island as the Dhammadeepa, the land where the Dhamma would be preserved and protected.

The *Mahavamsa* author Ven. Mahanama appears to have appointed himself as spokesman for the Buddha who had passed away approximately a thousand years before; via his epic poem, he declared that the Sinhala ethnic group was heir to the Teachings, the 'Buddha's chosen people' who would preserve, protect and propagate Buddhism for five thousand years. Since then, the Sinhalese have been brainwashed into believing and behaving as though they have exclusive ownership of Buddhism. 'Sri Lanka: the chosen land of the Buddha' is an obvious figment of Mahanama's overheated imagination that no one dares question.

Alarmingly, today, opportunistic Sinhala-Buddhist chauvinists, most of whom have never read the Mahavamsa or have either misunderstood or misinterpreted it, regard it as the blueprint for the way forward. In so doing, they are promoting the mainstreaming of bigotry, as the Mahavamsa is also given to racism and intolerance. For instance, Mahanama ends each chapter with the words "for the serene joy and emotion of the pious". However, his reference to Dutugemunu's murder of thousands of Tamils who he equates with "sinners and wild beasts" makes one question the author's understanding of "serene joy" and "pious".

Sadly, Mahanama's demeaning portrayal of the Tamil people of this land has resulted in an unfounded superiority complex and racist mindset amongst generations of chauvinistic Sinhala-Buddhists whose beliefs are based on a literal interpretation of the book. They regard it as the truth, the whole truth and nothing but the truth! By causing mistrust between the two communities, the Mahavamsa has also sapped the essence of what the Buddha taught. Furthermore, although the Mahawamsa is not a sacred Buddhist text, the Buddha and Buddhism figure prominently therein, perhaps due to Buddhism being part and parcel of this

81

country's history. In this land where, rich claims are held to the Buddha and Buddhism, one would expect to see and feel the Buddha's Teachings on tolerance and compassion personified.

Alas, what one sees is the exact opposite by distorting Buddhism through mythology and portraying the Buddha as a godlike figure given at times to performing magical feats and resorting to terror tactics, the author has, inadvertently or not, provided a base for Buddhism to be turned into a God-fearing 'religion' in Sri Lanka.

This is but one example: "To this great gathering of the Yakkas went the Blessed One and there in the midst of that assembly, hovering in the air over their heads, at the place of the future Mahiyangana Thupa, He struck terror to their hearts, by rain, storm, darkness and so forth. The Yakkas, overwhelmed by fear, besought the fearless Vanquisher to release them from fear. Then, when He had destroyed their terror . . . the Master preached them the doctrine." – William Geiger's translation of the Mahavamsa.

How can the Buddha, the Compassionate One, ever strike 'terror' in any heart? However, in a country rarely bereft of comedy, one still comes across, even amongst the 'academically qualified', those devoid of common sense and intelligence who are unable to distinguish between fact and fantasy. They reverently believe the myths pertaining to the Buddha contained in the Mahavamsa, including assertions of what the Buddha said and did right here, in

Dhammadeepa. Though the Mahavamsa was written very much after the Buddha's demise, there are some who even believe it was authored by the Buddha himself   a 'diary' of sorts   and therefore the unshakable truth! Some even confuse the Mahawamsa with the Tripitaka, the Buddhist scriptures.

So, what we have today is an utterly confused Sinhala-Buddhist progeny unable to distinguish between allegory, history, religion, myth, legend, and the philosophy of the Dhamma with misinterpretations of the Mahavamsa portraying the Buddha as a 'godlike' figure, including the many magical feats attributed to Him, Buddhist culture has turned Buddhism into a religion of worship which the average simple-minded Sinhala-Buddhist reverently accepts.

For example, there are those who sincerely believe that the mammoth indentation resembling a footprint on a boulder atop Adam's Peak ('Sri Pada' to Buddhists), to be that of the Buddha. This would be in keeping with the belief that the Buddha was as tall as, or perhaps even taller than, the renowned Avukana Buddha statue, which stands above 40 feet (12 meters) in height! Tall in wisdom they do not get.

Then, there is the 'Dalada Maligawa' in Kandy. Most Buddhists never cease to be awed by this place because they reverently believe the tooth relic housed within belonged to the Buddha.

Some adorn the 'tooth casket' with mounds of gold jewellery perhaps fervently believing they would earn merit to the value of the gold. The thought of donating this instead to feed and help the poor, homeless, sick, and the needy, which would be far more meritorious in the Buddha's eyes, has never crossed their self-serving minds.

Incidentally, there hangs a controversial question over the authenticity of this 'sacred tooth', given its size. But, then again, to those who believe the Buddha was as tall as the Avukana statue and had a giant foot as per the indentation on Adam's Peak, it would make sense that this abnormally large tooth had to be His. The annual Esala Perahera held in Kandy is yet another case in point. It has nothing to do with Philosophical Buddhism and everything to do with Cultural Buddhism. It is in fact an insult to the Buddha and the Dhamma. This senseless yet colourful and spectacular parade of animal abuse, at which the 'tooth relic' is displayed atop an elaborately-decorated, long-suffering elephant, has been nothing but an ego-boosting exercise for small-minded men, then and now. They too parade in this show with great pomposity, costumed like the kings of yore. This performance would be hilarious if not for the abuse of elephants involved.

The annual Esala Perahera therefore is no relation of Philosophical Buddhism, but bears all the hallmarks of Hinduism, which the

Buddha disassociated from his Dhamma! If the Buddha knew how those magnificent elephants are harassed, manacled and tortured for and during this 'parade', homeless dogs done away with to 'clean up' the city in preparation for the spectacle, all in the name of his tooth, he would be shattered and devastated. This is all done in the name of Buddhism, despite the Wise One having advised against revering or worshipping any part of his physical self, and his deification. Had he wanted otherwise, he would have left not just a tooth but his entire skeleton for his followers to venerate.

However, most find it is much easier to follow customs and traditions and perform the superficial culture-based rituals of a religion, than to absorb and uphold what the Great One asked of his followers to lead a life according to his teachings: the Dhamma! Thus, a mockery in the name of Buddhism continues to be performed by Sinhala-Buddhists of Dhammadeepa, Sri Lanka. Religious bigotry is common all over the world and Sri Lanka is no exception. In general, most Sinhala-Buddhists practice their 'religion' amongst themselves without harm to the rest of society. They keep their prejudices to themselves, and if they denigrate those of other religious groups, they do it covertly behind closed doors but overtly, hypocritically cordial to the Other.

The arrival of chauvinistic Sinhala-Buddhist political regimes, however, gradually changed the game over the years. By whipping up ethno-religious emotions for political gain, they legitimized this suppressed ugliness and brought it to the mainstream. It started with the late S. W. R. D. Bandaranaike and was exacerbated by the Rajapaksa regime. Under the Rajapaksa's, this malaise brimmed over to extreme proportions. We now have Sinhala-Buddhist thugs draped in saffron-robes masquerading as Buddhist monks and encouraging parents and teachers to teach their young how to look down upon and denigrate the Other, from an early age. This disturbing phenomenon burst forth in 2009, in post-war Sri Lanka. Today, Sinhala-Buddhists suffer from paranoia, and see 'demons' everywhere threatening Buddhism in Sri Lanka.

This could be attributed to the post-war political environment. After the successful elimination of LTTE terrorism, our warlords seemed to need another 'monster' from which to safeguard Sinhala-Buddhists. By doing so, they expect to keep the voter forever on edge and in constant fear, while reminding them ad infinitum that 'they' and 'they' alone have the ability to safeguard the country from threats such as the LTTE. Given the Sinhala-Buddhist psyche, this would be the perfect 'psyop' to keep the voter forever grateful to the Warlords who would keep them and their religion safe.

On the back of that sense of insecurity, Buddhist cultural symbols Buddha statues and temples started sprouting like mushrooms throughout the country. This phenomenon was mostly visible in areas populated by the Other – the Hindus, Christians and Muslims. This was the stamp of Sinhala-Buddhist supremacism. Not stopping there, they then went on to attack and destroy the places of religious worship of the Other. So, while overtly paying lip-service to the virtues of the Buddha, Dhamma, Sangha and religious harmony, the Sinhala-Buddhist warlords appeared to covertly give succor to prejudice by the thugs in saffron robes, allowing the latter to go on the rampage, terrorizing and intimidating the Other.

If one were to go by the Mahavamsa literally, the Sinhala race came about through bestiality; a physical union between a lion and a human princess, which makes the Sinhalese a subhuman race. Perhaps that explains why many a Sinhala man is so very lazy and whiles away his time in deep slumber, while the woman, the typical lioness, hunts for food to feed her young as well as the slumbering man. However, it seems far more plausible that the Sinhala ethnic group was a creation of the Buddhist monks of the Mahavihara, as opposed to dropping from the heavens above, as some of the delusional amongst my tribe, the Sinhalese, believe.

So, what did author Mahanama intend the Mahavamsa to be? It's certainly not an objective and balanced historical record of the people of Lanka of those times, both Sinhalese and Tamils, but more a glorification of the lion's descendants and the way forward for those who call themselves Sinhala-Buddhists today. The onus was on the Maha Sangha of this country who are supposed to be endowed with wisdom, to foresee the havoc the misinterpreted Mahavamsa would eventually create in this land. But they too are culpable in its promotion and propagation.

Firstly, had they been wise and selfless, they would have laid this historical book to rest, where it belongs: in the past. They would also not have confused Buddhist cultural practices and the philosophy of Buddhism, the Dhamma, but kept them wide apart. Thus, the Dhamma might have been propagated as the Buddha intended it to be. Buddhist monks would have been focussed on their calling and the Sinhala-Buddhists, a more enlightened and compassionate people. There are monks who fall into this category. Alas, they are only but a mere handful!

Had they done so, this land may have been a different place than the hellhole it has become today, especially for its minority communities and Sinhala moderates. Alas, racist Sinhala-Buddhist bigots amongst the clergy, laity and politicians have made the Mahavamsa into a scourge of this country, by crowning themselves with an unfounded superiority complex over the Other and turning it into a political guide and a tool for Sinhala-Buddhist politics.

Buddhist Culture Worshippers

The superficiality of the culture based 'brand' of Buddhism the majority of Sri Lankan Buddhists practice has made them extremely insecure about the survival of their religion in Sri Lanka. Thus they live in constant fear of the destruction of the 'concrete/clay/stone' symbols of their belief. The primary reason for this is their knowledge of the Buddha's teachings – the Dhamma, is near zero.

However, it is obvious to those Buddhists who are aware of 'impermanence' as preached by the Buddha that material objects, including symbols, are also impermanent, and vulnerable to destruction by natural phenomena or by humans over time. How can a religion based on symbols last?

This sense of insecurity harboured by Sinhala-Buddhists is not new to Sri Lanka. Its roots go back to the ancient times of the Cholas and more recently to pre-independent Ceylon, when the British introduced Christianity to the island. The likes of Anagarika Dhammapala, a Sinhala-Buddhist personified, claimed that Buddhism was being destroyed by the British and that Sinhala-Buddhists were being forced to convert to Christianity!

However, the reason for conversions   in addition to the degrading caste system (see Chapter 11) which made the task of the British missionaries so much easier   was the ritualisation of Buddhism in the country, placing Philosophical Buddhism on the back-burner ad infinitum and contributing to its erosion. None other than the Buddhist monks themselves were responsible for this.

Over the centuries, this was a concerted 'project' initiated and continued by them with no regard for the ethical cost of distorting and tarnishing the image of the Buddha's sacred Dhamma. Either their craving for increased numbers of gullible supporters amongst the laity made them blind or they didn't care about the long-term damage they were committing against the Dhamma. To keep their followers enthralled, some Buddhist monks conjured up all kinds of nonsensical rituals. Even occult practices (*hooniyang*) and astrology were introduced as part and parcel of Buddhism, to cater to the base instincts of their 'client base'. This process continues with impunity to date.

Over the years, these senseless cultural practices have taken precedence over and above the Philosophical Dhamma and have come to be regarded by all Cultural Buddhists as Buddhism. Though some of these rituals performed in the name of Buddhism are harmless in themselves, save for animal sacrifice and sorcery, they undermine the significance of the Buddha's Teachings.

Therefore, those who are aware of the moral principles of the Dhamma regard such practices as senseless and ridiculous, and hence do not practise them.

The majority of this country who label themselves 'Buddhists' are those who were born to families that have traditionally been Buddhist for generations. Thus they did not become Buddhists through an understanding and conviction of the Buddhist doctrine, but were simply 'born Buddhist' and labelled 'Buddhist'. To such, cultural practices comprise the entirety of their 'Buddhist religion'.

At its purest, the Buddha's Dhamma is too deep and complex a philosophy to be understood by the average, undisciplined and uneducated mind. As a result, it is greatly misunderstood and misinterpreted by the 'born Buddhist'. This is why most Buddhists in Sri Lanka tend to follow their own perception of Buddhism and unquestioningly emulate those before them, who regarded it as a god-worshipping religion with all the nonsensical cultural practices associated with it. They follow the herd instinct!

The Cultural Sinhala-Buddhist's idea of being a 'Good Buddhist' is confined to just a single day of the calendar month   Full Moon (Poya) day. As the done thing, they visit the temple, worship and heap flowers opposite the perceived image of the Buddha, light oil lamps, and drench the roots of an over-hydrated Bo tree within the temple premises. Then they parrot off the Five Precepts with no intention of abiding by them. Most have no idea of what the precepts mean!

Thus, on this very 'holy' Full Moon (Poya) day, they piously perform 'religious rituals' reminiscent of those from Hinduism. Amongst the most commonly practiced are the following:

•   Draped in white, they dutifully make a bee-line to a temple, similar to the practice of Christians attending church on Sundays and Muslims the mosque on Fridays and piously recite the Five Precepts and other Buddhist verses, as in 'praying' to the Buddha's 'Godly image'.

•   Offer flowers, usually stolen from a neighbour's garden, to a clay, plaster or stone statue perceived to be His image.

•   Light oil lamps expecting more merit.

•   Drench the roots of a 'Bo tree' (Bodhi Puja) with pots of water encouraging tree-rot, simply because He attained Enlightenment under one.

The Five Precepts are the basic code of ethics which the Buddhist laity is expected to abide by according to the Dhamma. But to many Cultural Sinhala-Buddhists, these are mere mutterings that cease to hold any value or significance the moment they are uttered, and beyond the temple gates!

Thus, practice of the Five Precepts – abstinence from alcohol, lying, stealing, sexual misconduct and murder/killing – is confined only to Poya Day, after which, convinced and content that they have accumulated sufficient merit to see them through all their misdeeds until the dawn of the next Poya Day, life returns to normal.

In Buddhism, the flower symbolises life's impermanence (*anicca*): 'Just as this flower fades and decays, so will our bodies fade and decay'. But to the average Sinhala-Buddhist who knows not its deep meaning, placing flowers opposite a Buddha image is merely a method of obtaining merit.

The lighting of an oil lamp represents the light of wisdom illuminating the darkness of ignorance. But again, to the average unilluminated Sinhala-Buddhist unaware of its deep meaning, it is merely a way to obtain merit.

The Cultural Sinhala-Buddhist drenches the roots of a 'Bo tree' (Bodhi Puja) with pots of water expecting the 'holy tree' under which 'God Buddha' attained 'godliness' to bestow merit upon them. During trying times, unable to accept the consequences of their own karmic actions, they expect the tree to provide deliverance from their misery.

Furthermore, the Buddha never asked his followers to invite home Buddhist monks to lunch (alms-giving) in order to transfer merit to the departed so that they may go straight to heaven or attain Nirvana. If this was so, even rapists, murderers, child molesters et al, might be born as angels in heaven or attain nirvana, courtesy of almsgivings. The Buddha never made any such promises to his followers!

Neither did the Buddha promise that by engaging in these nonsensical practices one would receive deliverance from ill health, loss of employment and wealth and other miseries arising from a 'bad period', or merit for their departed ones.

All of this is done for reasons of propriety, foolishness and selfishness; to gain merit that will reduce the ill-effects of negative karma. It never occurs to these adherents to question how a tree, clay, concrete or stone object could grant pardon or merit. They perform these rituals with no understanding of why they do it, except the fervent belief that they are practising 'Buddhism'.

Another hypocritical and ridiculous practice amongst the usually meat-eating Sinhala-Buddhists is to go vegetarian or vegan on Poya day. This they believe will grant them more merit, further strengthen their chances of a one-way ticket to Nirvana or a more luxurious rebirth; given their pitiful mindset, Cultural Buddhists would much rather prefer the latter!

A related misconception is that the Buddha prohibited his followers from consuming meat, which is commonly believed to be banned in Buddhism! On the contrary, the Buddha did not 'prohibit or ban' his followers from doing anything including consuming meat, but advised them to accept with gratitude anything, including meat, offered by one in good faith. However, the Buddha did caution his followers against seeking meat, as it contributes to the destruction of a life. Sensible Buddhists who refrain from consuming meat do so either for compassionate, health or ethical reasons.

Thus, in typical Sinhala-Buddhist style, commercial establishments in Sri Lanka are banned by the State from selling meat on Poya days. Strangely the ban does not apply to seafood; as perhaps they believe it grows on trees. The ban also applies to the sale of alcohol. Nevertheless, Sinhala Buddhists are not banned from storing as much meat as they require in their refrigerators in the days preceding this 'sacred' day and stocking up sufficient quantities of alcohol to see them through the day of prohibition.

Sinhala-Buddhists are most often amongst the first customers at meat stalls and taverns before the day of 'prohibition' dawns. So, for whose benefit and for what purpose are such prohibitions imposed? Who is trying to fool whom? Isn't this nothing more than Sinhala-Buddhist state-sponsored hypocrisy!

Yet another practice of the Cultural Sinhala-Buddhists, perhaps to display their ethno-religious identity on their sleeve, is to bandage their wrists with multi-coloured strands of thread instead of the customary three folds of white cotton thread, the Pirith Nool. This is particularly common amongst our Sinhala-Buddhist VIPs. This could be either to draw attention to their superior ethno-religious identity and authority over the 'Other' or to ensure ludicrous 'divine protection' against the negative karma accumulated through their evil deeds. It also could be a combination of both.

None of these above-mentioned ritualistic practices have anything to do with Philosophical Buddhism. But the Sinhala-Buddhist engages in all these as it is the idée recue and with the fervent hope they will be pardoned from and insured against suffering, as well as gain merit to acquire more of whatever they desire. Hence Cultural Buddhism is practiced by most Sinhala-Buddhists as a 'religion' that satisfies a basic human need; divine assistance in the hour of need and greed.

The root cause of this phenomenon may be attributed to the absence of a God in Buddhism to appeal to in times of crisis as in other faiths. Thus the Buddha's theory of karma (cause and effect), the fundamental factor of the Dhamma, has no place in Sri Lanka's Cultural Sinhala-Buddhism, for it offers no divine salvation in times of need.

A base instinct in the average human being requires a supernatural power to cling to and look up to in the face of crisis, and in this regard, the Dhamma fails to deliver. So the first urge of such a Sinhala-Buddhist in crisis is to run to the temple, pile flowers in front of Buddha statues, light oil lamps, pour gallons of water on a Bo tree and conduct other nonsensical rituals.

When all this fails to deliver or for further insurance, they next take off to a Hindu kovil, smash coconuts, sacrifice animals, pray for miracles or curse and damn to hell, their mortal enemies. Then, for further measure, they run to a Christian/Catholic church to light candles and plead to God, Jesus, Virgin Mary and all the Saints for help. Some even appeal to Sai Baba's photograph! A 'privileged' few even visit a mosque; I have no idea what they do there.

At all these places, deals are struck with various Gods through vows (bribes) on a quid pro quo basis; you-scratch-my-back-and-I'll-scratch-yours type of deal.

This is not to say that there aren't Sinhalese both amongst the Buddhist clergy and the laity who don't practice Philosophical Buddhism according to the Dhamma but that the majority, unfortunately, from the Mahanayakes and politicians downward observe the *differentia specifica* of Theravada Buddhism: Cultural Sinhala-Buddhism!

In this so-called thrice-blessed Dhammadeepa 2,500 years ago; the Buddhist clergy of this country transformed the Buddhist doctrine into an 'ethnic' religion of the Sinhala people, and propagated it as such. Thus, over the years, Buddhists of this country have been misled, misguided, led astray and lied to by many self-serving amongst our Cultural Buddhist clergy for their own benefit.

During the Buddha's time, monks were mendicants who walked around barefoot begging for alms. This was the Theravada Buddhist practice called *piṇḍapāta*. Not so in Sri Lanka anymore, where over the years Cultural Sinhala-Buddhism has become *sine qua non* and validated as the religion of the Sinhala-Buddhist state. Largely for convenience, political leverage, benefit and welfare of irreligious monks, politicians and the laity, the practice of *piṇḍapāta* has also ceased. Though a mere handful do still wander around begging for alms on foot, it is a very rare sight.

For this, the Buddhist laity is mostly to be blamed, as they have failed to respect the monastic conventions of a Buddhist monk's lifestyle by absorbing them into their lay involvements, thus tempting them away from the Vinaya Pitaka; the disciplinary code for Buddhist monks. Gone are the days, when monks were ascetics confined to a monastic life. Today, no event, either of personal, national, political or other significance, is complete without the prominent patronage of Buddhist monks.

Thus, Buddhist monks gradually but steadily weaned themselves away from a life of mendicancy by ingraining themselves in the lives, psyche, social and political fabric of Sinhala-Buddhist society, who in turn welcomed these 'messengers' of 'God Buddha' with open arms. Today, the demand for their 'services' especially at alms-givings, officiating at weddings etc., is so great that they even maintain diaries, to give out appointments for invitations.

May one ask if the same degree of 'merit' can be gained or granted by feeding the hungry amongst the poor laity, or starving animals instead, or is it only the saffron-robed 'messengers of God Buddha' who are able to grant visas to heaven or Nirvana?

What most monks of today would not admit voluntarily is that no matter what the living do for their dead, and how many expensive 'alms-giving' ceremonies they hold and gifts they give, nothing or no one, including the saffron-robed, can change the course of one's karmic path to ensure a better 'next birth'; the living simply cannot transfer merit to the dead, and that is the hard truth of the Dhamma.

But the gullible laity continue to believe that the more you feed and spoil the saffron-robed 'messengers' most of them overindulged and unworthy of the robes they wear the more 'merit' they and their dearly departed would receive!

Today, Buddhist monks who have deviated from the Vinaya Pitaka have become diabolic jacks of many trades. One of them is occult practices a total affront to the sacred Dhamma! In a pathetic attempt to justify this economically-viable 'business', these monks meddling in witchcraft have lumped it together with the cultural practice of Bodhi Pooja, defining this senseless yet harmless ritual as an occult practice. Thus Bodhi Pujas are performed to earn profits, power and destroy enemies.

Since time immemorial, Buddhist monks, contrary to the very teachings of the Buddha, have been involved in witchcraft, the casting of horoscopes, and astrology; the latter borrowed from Hinduism, as is the case with all practices denounced by the Buddha. This transformation by Buddhist monks into ritual and occult practicing 'specialists' has become a socio-psychological scourge today.

Many amongst these Cultural Buddhist clergy are monks in name only, as they have deviated from the path of all that entails a monastic life and violated the Vinaya Pitaka with impunity. And most of those who join the Buddhist Order of monks today do so not because of their understanding of and commitment to the Dhamma, but to take advantage of the numerous benefits accorded to those draped in saffron robes.

Except for a handful, they appear to have no idea of or regard for what the Vinaya Pitaka stands for. It's not too late for the sincere and good amongst the Buddhist clergy to cleanse their order by showing the door to the charlatans. The support of the laity is imperative in this regard, as a monk would find it impossible to lead the spiritual life he is meant for without their cooperation and respect for monastic conventions. For this, the laity must be aware of what the Vinaya Pitaka stands for and establish a relationship with monks accordingly.

Hopefully, this would give rise to a renewed relationship of mutual respectability and sincerity between the Buddhist clergy and the laity, and repair the damage done to the image of Buddhism in this country, even in the distant future.

The Curse of the Caste System

Long before Sri Lanka became a colony of the West, Buddhism and Hinduism were the predominant faiths of the Sinhalese and Tamils respectively. These equations changed after the arrival of the colonial powers.

However, was colonialism the only reason for the shifts of religious allegiance? What made it so easy for the Sinhalese who were originally Buddhists to turn to other religions? Of course, the colonialists favoured their converts. But it wasn't the only reason; the demeaning and deplorable caste system of Sri Lanka was as much to blame!

Sinhala documents of yore are replete with references of the elaborately-ordered caste hierarchy of Buddhist Sri Lanka. For example, in the 2nd century BC, King Dutugemenu had his son, Saliya, exiled because he married an 'outcast', Asokamala. In the 11th century AD, King Vijaybahu denied 'low-caste' Sinhalese access to venerate the 'Buddha's footprint' at Sri Pada. Instead they had to worship from a terrace much further below the site.

The caste system denounced and rejected by the Buddha has been upheld by none other than the Buddhist clergy of the so-called 'supreme' Radala and Govigama castes. The division of the Buddhist monastic order into *nikayas*, factions based on caste divisions, was pioneered by none other than these hypocritical, 'high caste' Govigama and Radala Buddhist monks of the Siam Nikaya, who refuse Buddhists deemed 'low-caste' access to their temples even today. In the eyes of the Philosophical Buddhist, this amounts to blatant sacrilege and a downright insult to the Buddha and the Dhamma!

The Siam Nikaya, which grants higher ordination only to those of the Radala and Govigama castes, has two major divisions: the Malwatte and Asgiriya chapters. There are other divisions within these two units. The Maha Nayakas or Chief Monks of these 'organisations' founded on Govigama and Radala aristocracy and caste-based politics in 1764, govern them like self-appointed deputies of the Buddha, while practicing and propagating the very antithesis of what the Noble One preached and stood for.

A quick look at the history of the monastic orders in Sri Lanka will shed light on the development of caste-based Buddhism in Sri Lanka. By the mid-18th century, Buddhism was in crisis in the country. Higher ordination of Buddhist monks had once again become extinct, the fourth such occurrence in five hundred years. During the reigns of kings Vimaladharmasuriya I and II of Kandy (1591-1707), the Buddhist monastic order was reestablished, but did not last long because the Vinaya Pitaka had been virtually abandoned, as is happening today. At the time, certain 'Buddhist monks' known as Gaṇinnānsēlās owned property, married, had children, and lived in private residences. Déjà vu! Talk about history repeating itself!

During the reign of Kirti Sri Rajasinha of Kandy (1747 1782), Weliwita Sri Saranankara Thero (1698 1778) invited the Thai Buddhist monk Upali Thera to visit Kandy. He re-established the Buddhist order in Sri Lanka in 1753, with a Thai identity as the 'Siam Nikaya'. However, approximately eleven years later, in 1764, some within the Siam Nikaya started placing restrictions on who should and should not receive *upasampada* (higher ordination). Thus began the despicable trend of granting *upasampada* only to those of the Radala and Govigama castes, and it has been a 'tradition' ever since.

Reportedly, the practice of ordaining monks based on the caste system came into being with Kirti Sri Rajasinha having a baffling experience; he came across a Buddhist monk supposedly from a low-caste who stood up from his seat and bowed to the king. Since a monk is not expected to bow his head to any lay person whatever his social standing, the king had been troubled by the experience and, therefore, requested the Chief Monks of the Malwatte temple to refrain from ordaining men of low-caste birth.

However, it seems more plausible that the caste-conscious among the Kandyan Radala and Govigama communities felt it was *infra dig* to bow to an ordained man of a lower caste, hence the refusal to grant higher ordination to those deemed as of a low caste!

As a result of the policy of exclusivity adopted by the Siam Nikaya, Buddhists especially from the coastal areas of the country were denied access to *upasampada* (higher ordination). This forced those of the Karava, Salagama and Durava castes to seek ordination in Myanmar. Thus was born the Amarapura Nikaya around 1800, named after Amarapura, the former capital of Myanmar. Unlike the Siam Nikaya, the Amarapura Nikaya does not practise caste discrimination and thus welcomes all those who were shown the door by the caste-conscious Siam Nikaya.

It was to the Amarapura Nikaya that my erudite Guru, Ven. Piyadassi Maha Thera, who taught me the Dhamma, belonged.

Further, in 1864, the modernist Ramanna Nikaya was founded, rejecting caste as a qualification for entry into the Sangha. This was how the Buddha meant it to be. Most forest monasteries come under the umbrella of this order, where the strictest of meditation practices continue to date. Many simple old Buddhist traditions, such as palm leaf umbrellas, alms bowls and the covering of both shoulders while begging for alms, are preserved and practised by the Buddhist monks of the Ramanna Nikaya.

To the laity, the caste-based politics of the Siam Nikaya can be very confusing. I recall a virtual life-changing drama that I witnessed as a child, the emotional scar of which remains with me to date. My grandmother in Kandy held an alms-giving on a grand scale at our ancestral home. All the 'high-caste' bigwigs from the Malwatte and Asgiriya chapters and their entourages from their Siam Nikaya were invited, along with a dear and close friend of our family, the most Ven. Piyadassi Maha Thera of the Amarapura Nikaya.

Suddenly, there erupted a ruckus. The 'high-caste' monks had refused to partake of alms together with their 'low-caste' counterpart, the Ven. Piyadassi Maha Thera of the Amarapura Nikaya. The entire household was thrown into a quandary, but peace was restored when Ven. Piyadassi Maha Thera agreed to partake of alms away from the rest. Much to the embarrassment of my poor grandmother, special arrangements were made to accommodate Ven. Piyadassi Maha Thera of the 'low caste' Amarapura Nikaya.

It is through such incidents that I as a child first learnt of the repugnant caste system in Sri Lanka that boasts a 2,500-year culture, courtesy of the Sinhala-Buddhist Mahanayakes of the Malwatte and Asgiriya chapters! Had I been my grandmother, I would have kicked out the whole lot, except for my guru and friend of the family Ven. Piyadassi Maha Thera.

Is it any wonder then that Buddhists deemed 'low caste' would turn to more tolerant and compassionate religions, which unlike Cultural Sinhala-Buddhism offer no place to caste, creed and ethnicity? To the Hindus of India, the age-old tradition of the caste system was of utmost importance. However, it was of utter repugnance to the Buddha who strongly condemned the degradation of humanity it entailed.

The Buddha very specifically stated that there are no different species among human beings, as is found in fauna and flora, and thereby threw open the door to liberation of the entire human race, devoid of caste. The Buddha welcomed people from all walks of life, castes and classes into his Order and united those he deemed fit to lead the holy life. They abandoned their former identity, including their names, castes and clans, and came to be known as members of a single community   the Sangha. They sat, ate, meditated and slept together as equals, and some went on to distinguish themselves. Equality was a vital cornerstone of the 'Buddha Sasana'! Today, save a few, where does one find such equanimity amongst our Sinhala-Buddhist monks?

Meanwhile, it is the Amaparapura Nikaya that has produced the majority of erudite Buddhist monks whose sincere mission has been to propagate the Philosophical Dhamma as opposed to cultural, caste-based and politically-influenced Sinhala-Buddhism. Beacons amongst them were Palane Vajiragnana Thera, Narada Maha Thera, and Piyadassi Maha Thera of the Amarapura Nikaya.

There were others such as Weligama Sri Sumangala Thera, Madihe Pannaseeha Thera, Balangoda Ananda Maitreya Thera and Gangodawila Soma Thera. However, their focus was not entirely on the path of the Dhamma because politics and 'national interest' clouded their vision.

Ven. Palane Vajiragnana Thera (1878 – 1955)

Palane Vajiragnana Thera was a distinguished scholar Buddhist monk who founded the renowned Siri Vajiraramaya temple in Bambalapitiya, Colombo. His profound knowledge of the Buddhist Scriptures (Tripitaka) and his views on the Dhamma and monastic discipline were highly respected both by his disciples and the laity. Thus, his was regarded as the final word on the subject.

When he was twenty-seven years old, he was made a member of the prestigious Pracheena Bhasopakara Samitiya on the recommendation of Ven. Hikkaduwe Sri Sumangala Mahanayaka Thera due to his erudition, scholarship, and near perfection in following the monastic rules laid out in the Vinaya Pitaka. His foresightedness in all his undertakings earned him recognition above all his seniors. In 1918, aged forty three, he was elected the

Mahānāyaka (Chief Prelate) of the Amarapura Sri Dharmarakshita sect, a position he held for thirty seven years until his demise in 1955.

The history of the Vajirārāmaya temple is synonymous with this erudite monk. He transformed one of its preaching halls into a world-renowned Buddhist institution. He also formed a community of monks who later became prominent Buddhist missionaries spreading the revered teachings of the Buddha Dhamma worldwide. And he encouraged younger generations of Buddhists to be good citizens and advocated a virtuous society through his writings and sermons.

The Ven. Thera laid great emphasis on following the monastic rules of discipline contained in the Pātimokkha, the basic code of monastic discipline in Theravada Buddhism. Due to this, the monks of the Vajirārāmaya stood out from the rest and were easily recognised. Among their notable features was an alms-bowl for partaking meals and the use of herbal dyes in their robes. This unique hue from the dye became known as the 'Vajirārāma-colour'. Rules and procedures pertaining to the Vajirārāmaya temple and the monks ordained by him were laid down in the Vajirārāma Katikavata in 1940.

Ven. Narada Maha Thera (1898 – 1983)

Ven. Narada Maha Thera is undoubtedly one of the greatest Buddhist missionaries of the 20th Century. When the Ven. Pelene Vajiragnana Maha Nayaka Thera met the young Sumanapala Perera for the first time, he saw in the teenager great potential to make his mark in the Theravada Buddhist world. So, on his 18th birthday, Sumanapala was ordained at Vajiraramaya and thus took on the identity 'Narada'. Two years later, he attained upasampada (higher ordination).

Ven. Narada had the good fortune of having no less than the Most Ven. Pelene Vajiragnana Maha Nayaka Thera as his mentor. As an external student, Ven. Narada studied Ethics and Philosophy at the University College, Colombo. As a young monk of only twenty one years of age, he showed exceptional intellectual prowess matched by an equal degree of spiritual sincerity. With the mature guidance and advice of Dr. Cassius Pereira (later Ven. Kassappa Thera of Vajiraramaya Temple), Ven. Narada mastered the English language to perfection and went on to become an eloquent and powerful speaker. He captivated the minds of the English-educated Buddhists with his lucid and refined sermons.

At the age of thirty one, Ven. Narada ventured beyond the shores of the land of his birth for the first time. When the Mulagandhakuti Vihara in Sarnath, India, was completed in 1929, a Sri Lankan delegation including Ven. Narada was invited for its opening ceremony. Ven. Narada was granted the honour of conducting all proceedings at this historic function, which was graced by Pandit Jawaharlal Nehru whom Ven. Narada met for the first time.

During his fifty years of missionary work, Ven. Narada travelled widely until his demise in 1983. His most successful missions in Asia were in Indonesia, Nepal, Singapore and Vietnam. In many a country, he was the first Theravada Buddhist monk to have visited in recent times. In Indonesia, he is remembered as the first Theravada monk to have set foot in the country in approximately four hundred and fifty years. Ven. Narada considered Vietnam as his second home, and during the height of the Vietnamese war, he did not abandon his Vietnamese followers. As an Ambassador of the Dhamma, he led over six Dhammaduta missions to Nepal. Ven. Narada was highly respected by the Nepalese Royalty and this further strengthened the establishment of the Theravada Sangha in Nepal.

Ven. Narada visited Africa in 1947. This goodwill mission lasted over a month and took him to Mombasa, Dar es Salaam, Zanzibar and Nairobi. Commenting on the trip, he is said to have stated, "During my stay, I emphasized the need for Christian neighbourliness, Muslim brotherhood, Hindu oneness, and Buddhist maitrī (benevolence)."

Ven. Narada fitted the role of a missionary monk to perfection as he had the erudition, piety and composure as well as a perfect command of the English language. Thus he was able to interpret the most profound teachings of the Buddha simply and eloquently. Some of his books are written in English; *The Buddha and His Teachings*, a translation of the 'Dhammapada', and *Buddhism in a Nutshell* have been translated into several languages. They are amongst the clearest, detailed introductions to the fundamental teachings of the Buddha. He made the doctrine and the concepts which form the common bedrock of Theravada Buddhism available in English.

Ven. Piyadassi Maha Thera (1914 – 1998)

Piyadassi Maha Thera is internationally renowned as an erudite preacher of the Dhamma in both Sinhala and English.

At the age of twenty he entered the Buddhist Order and mastered the Philosophy of the Dhamma under the erudite scholar monk Ven. Palane Vajiragnana Thera. Later he received his higher ordination under the tutorship of his mentor.

He was educated at Nalanda College, Colombo; at the University of Sri Lanka; and at the Center for the Study of World Religions, Harvard University. His close associate was Ven. Narada Maha Thera, the senior-most pupil of Ven. Palane Vajiragnana Thera, whose invaluable influence contributed towards his younger counterpart's dedication and determination towards serving the Sasana.

Ven. Piyadassi continued with his studies while living a frugal life; studying by candlelight, walking the streets practicing *pindapatha* for his food, and sleeping on a mat on the floor at the Vajiraramaya Temple.

Although he had no traditional Pirivena education, he obtained a degree in Vidya Visarada from the University of Ceylon. In 1964, the Asia Foundation awarded him a scholarship to follow a course of study in Comparative Religion at Harvard University, USA. His stay in that country afforded him the practical experience and opportunity for his future role as a great preacher of the Dhamma, and he delivered lectures on the Dhamma at various educational institutions and universities.

Ven. Piyadassi was one of the world's most eminent Buddhist monks having travelled widely. Through his international Dhammaduta travels, he took the message of the Dhamma from the East to the West and to the far corners of the world; Ghana, Brazil, Iceland, Finland, Trinidad, Peru, Venezuela, Jamaica, Hungary, Fiji Islands, Zambia, Canadian, Newfoundland etc. In this field alone, his services were outstanding. He also had the advantage of a writing style that had universal appeal, and he was both a member of the Board of Management and editor of the

Sinhala publications of the Buddhist Publication Society, until his death.

As a writer, he authored numerous books in both Sinhala and English. His internationally-acclaimed *Buddha's Ancient Path* is a thorough exposition of the Four Noble Truths and the Eightfold Noble Path. The lively explanations are illuminated with many appropriate stories and quotations from the Buddha.

In Sri Lanka, Ven. Piyadassi became a popular preacher and his name became synonymous with the Dhamma. He accepted invitations for sermons from the richest and most powerful to the poorest of the poor. He also rendered benevolent services to prisoners, routinely visiting prisons throughout the island to preach the Dhamma to the misguided, languishing behind bars.

He was indeed a true Bhikku in every sense of the word!

Ven. Dr. Walpola Rahula Thera (1907   1997)

Alas from the 'high-caste' Siam Nikaya there is only one Buddhist monk that comes to mind and worthy of mention, Ven. Dr. Walpola Rahula Thera, one of the most celebrated Buddhist monks of Sri Lanka and of the entire Buddhist world.

He seemed to have had no value or regard for titles such as 'Venerable', 'Doctor', 'Professor' or 'Thera', as he went by the plain and simple identity of 'Walpola Rahula'. He also appears not to have had any regard for the nikaya to which he belonged, as he never referred to it, thus seemingly not wanting to be associated with it.

Ven. Walpola Rahula entered the Buddhist monastic order at the age of thirteen and received his education at Vidyalankara Pirivena and at the University of Ceylon, now the University of Colombo. He studied further at the University of Calcutta and at Sorbonne University. His subjects of study included Sinhala, Pali, Sanskrit, Buddhism, History and Philosophy.

In 1964, he became the first Buddhist monk to hold a professorial position at a Western university; the Northwestern University in Illinois, USA. In 1966, Ven. Rahula became the Vice Chancellor of the University of Sri Jayewardenepura. He did much to improve the university, although his tenure of office was short.

His contribution to the advancement of Buddhism was tremendous. As an accomplished writer, he published numerous books on Buddhism in Sinhala, English and French, the most renowned being *What the Buddha Taught*. Many regard this book as having connected them with the Buddha's teachings for the very first time, and refer to it whenever life's challenges become unbearable. It focusses on the true nature of the Dhamma and explains its teachings rather than concentrating on the persona of the Buddha.

Walpola Rahula of the caste-conscious Siyam Nikaya was akin to a lotus bloom in a pool of mud; what a contrast he was to the marauding Galagoda Aththe Gnanasara, also of the Siam Nikaya!

In summation, Sinhala-Buddhism was ordered on the basis of the caste system which the Buddha vehemently rejected, and many Sinhalese in disgust, converted to other religions which regarded all mankind as equal. Even in this day and age, many Buddhist monks of Sri Lanka, in the name of tradition, continue to uphold the repugnant caste system far more than the laity. To enshrine caste as a tradition in the Buddha Sasana is not just a blasphemous mockery of the Vinaya Pitaka, but a preposterous insult to the Buddha.

The practice of Sinhala-Buddhism reverses the Teachings and thus undermines and attempts to destroy the very essence of the Dhamma. Isn't that a downright violation of Chapter II of Article 9 enshrined in our Constitution that specifically states, "The Republic of Sri Lanka shall give to Buddhism the foremost place and accordingly it shall be the duty of the State to protect and foster the Buddha Sasana"?

In this context, isn't the Maha Sanga of the so-called Radala and Govigama Siam Nikaya chapters claiming to be the 'sole protectors' of Buddhism in this so-called 'Cradle of Theravada Buddhism Sri Lanka' aka 'Dhammadeepa', committing a form of blatant treason with impunity? Shouldn't 'protecting' the Sasana from these hypocrites be the place to start?

Their pathetic justification that it is a time-honoured tradition established on the orders of a Sinhala King, Kirthi Sri Rajasinghe, a man drunk with power, only proves their utter foolishness, lack of understanding and respect for the Buddha and the Dhamma. What a shallow-minded lot these Sinhala-Buddhist monks and laity are! In the name of Buddhism, these monks are adhering to rules laid down by a megalomaniac king, as opposed to the Dhamma of the Compassionate One, the Buddha!

"Birth makes not a man an outcast, Birth makes not a man a Brahmin; Actions make a man an outcast, Actions make a man a Brahmin." (Sutta-nipâta, 142)

Child Ordination is Child Abuse

As a mother, this has to be one of the most emotionally-challenging topics I have ever written on; child ordination! I see a son of mine in each child samanera (novice Buddhist monk)!

At an alms-giving ceremony I attended, there were many such samaneras of varying ages. Some as young as seven or eight years of age, while some were of pubertal age. The little ones with shaven heads and thin bodies swathed in saffron robes much too large for them, sat on the floor with their elders looking utterly bewildered. It was hard to miss the mélange of expressions on their innocent faces; sheer wonder coupled with confusion and mischief as they watched their lay counterparts run wild, having the time of their lives despite the 'solemn' event, the significance of which held no water for them.

One of these 'miniature monks' in particular had his gaze fixed longingly on a teddy bear which a child of an invitee was cuddling lovingly. Another on a group of little boys playing with a train set. Those in their mid- to late-teens gazed appreciatively at the pretty young girls around, before quickly hiding their blushing faces behind their over-sized palm-leaf fans, when frowned upon by a disapproving adult monk. It was obvious that these young children thrust into monkhood were oblivious to the fact that they had been robbed of their childhood, for no fault of their own!

In all their innocence, how would they know that their young lives would change forever when asked to commit themselves to ordination with a promise to renounce all that they held dear: "Venerable Sir, I respectfully ask you to ordain me as a novice monk, in order that I may be free from the cycle of existence and attain Nibbana"?

How can a seven-year-old understand what it means to be 'free from the cycle of existence and attain Nibbana'? Can this little child realise that he can no longer be carried, hugged and kissed by his mother, and seek her maternal warmth and security when struck with a fever, or frightened by a nightmare, thunder or lightning?

Further, these child-samaneras are committed to observe the 'Ten Precepts' as training rules:

- I undertake to abstain from harming or taking life;

- I undertake to abstain from taking what is not given;

- I undertake to abstain from any sexual contact;

- I undertake to abstain from false speech;

- I undertake to abstain from the use of intoxicants;

- I undertake to abstain from taking food after midday;

- I undertake to abstain from dancing, singing, music or any kind of entertainment;

- I undertake to abstain from the use of garlands, perfumes, unguents and adornments;

- I undertake to abstain from using luxurious seats; and

- I undertake to abstain from accepting and holding money.

Save for some, the rest of these 'rules' are those that even an un-ordained child brought up in a morally-healthy family environment abides by. So why must a child be ordained a Buddhist monk to abide by such rules? Is it because the parents of such children are morally bankrupt?

Furthermore, is it in the best interest of an ordained child's mental and physical development to make him 'abstain from taking food after midday?' Do those who promote and encourage child-ordination realise or give a damn, about the physical and mental damage caused to a growing young child by depriving him of nourishment, for more than half a day?

Also, is it ethically correct to commit such a young child to a life-long sentence of deprivation not of his choosing: married life, family life, celibacy and a whole host of other taboos, at an age when he cannot understand the high price he has been called upon to pay? The Buddha himself followed his chosen path according to his own free will; no one forced him to do so. And this too he did, at the age of twenty-nine, after having married and fathered a child.

The traditional myth regarding the Buddha having ordained his seven-year-old son seems too farfetched, given his enlightened status. Thus, it seems more likely that our Sinhala-Buddhist monks concocted this fallacy to entice and brainwash gullible parents of young sons to hand over their offspring to add numbers to their flock. Hence, according to this myth, it is believed, that it is a meritorious act to 'donate' their young sons to the temple. What moral right do parents of such trusting and innocent children have to commit them to a life-sentence of deprivation? Isn't this blatant child-abuse?

According to the laws of Sri Lanka, a person cannot be less than eighteen-years of age to marry, vote or to obtain a driving license. So why doesn't the same law apply to child ordination?

If this is not child abuse, what does one call it?

Why Buddhists 'Donate' their sons to the Temple

Malefic Horoscopes

Astrology is not a facet of the Dhamma, but one of the many traditional beliefs and customs borrowed by Sinhala-Buddhists from Hinduism. Sometimes, parents are made to believe that a son born under the 'wrong stars' (malefic horoscope) must be 'donated' to the temple. This, they believe, will ward off the ill-effects that the bad luck of the child will have on the rest of the family.

> *'The fool may watch for lucky days,*
> *Yet luck he shall always miss,*
> *The luck itself is luck's own star,*
> *What can mere stars achieve?*
> – The Buddha

The Buddha, as stated above, did not advocate one to live by movements of the stars, and our Sangha know this only too well. However, many prefer to overlook the Teachings for their own purposes!

Poverty

Acute poverty is a reason why some parents 'donate' their young sons to the temple. When these poor parents find it hard to make ends meet, the only option available to them is the temple. Here, the question that arises is whether it is ethically correct for such children of the poor to be committed to a life-sentence of monastic life for lack of funds to feed and educate them?

Although the temple provides his food, clothing, shelter and education, is he also protected against the dangers such as sexual abuse by the pedophiles amongst the clergy? What could his poor parents do if their young sons were victims of such evils, except to turn a blind-eye due to their circumstances? What of the long-term psychological damage caused to such children?

Furthermore, why cannot the affluent landlords and businessmen amongst the Buddhist monks and laity, if there are any benevolent among them, help these poor families to keep their sons within their family unit? But then again, there may be those who want to keep these family's poor to ensure a constant 'supply', of 'soldiers' to the Cultural Sinhala-Buddhist 'army'!

National Child Protection Authority

What in all this incidence of child-abuse does the role of the 'National Child Protection Authority (NCPA)' of Sri Lanka, play?

According to their website:

"Sri Lanka, as a member State of the United Nations, was a signatory to the Child Rights Convention (CRC) in the year 1990 and ratified it on 12 July 1991. This was followed by the preparation of a Children's Charter approved by the Cabinet of Ministers, and the establishing of a National Monitory Committee charged with the responsibility to monitor the CRC and also report to the international CRC committee when required. In December 1996, the Presidential Task Force on Child Protection was appointed. This body recommended a number of Legal amendments and administrative reforms, which were included in the report of Presidential Task Force.

One of the most important recommendations of the Presidential Task Force was the establishment of the National Child Protection Authority (NCPA), by ACT No.50 of 1998 under the Presidential Secretariat. In the year 2006, a separate ministry was formed by the incumbent president of Sri Lanka to establish a proper protection and welfare mechanism for children and women and NCPA is under the purview of the Ministry of Child Development and Women`s Affairs."

The website further states:

The NCPA VISION; to create a child friendly and protective environment for children.

Its MISSION; to ensure children are free from all forms of abuse.

All laudable, well and good, but what about those children of Sri Lanka subjected to ordination? Are they not 'children' as per the NCPA's definition of a child? Does the NCPA reach out to these young ordained children or doesn't it come under their 'purview'? Does the NCPA raise public awareness and influence policies and practices that affect the lives and welfare of these ordained-children as well? Or is it none of their business?

Does the NCPA work together with relevant authorities/systems such as the police, healthcare, legal, education, communication, media, political and all sectors of society to look into problems faced by the child-samaneras as well?

Or don't they care? Does the NCPA contribute to and work towards strengthening and networking with global child protection systems, in ensuring that the voices of these child-Samaneras are also heard? Or do they not matter?

Does the NCPA not regard these ordained children as children of Sri Lanka? The NCPA VISION: to create a child friendly and protective environment for children.

Its MISSION: to ensure children are free from all forms of abuse.

All laudable, well and good, but what about those children of Sri Lanka subjected to ordination? Are they not 'children' as per the NCPA's definition of a 'child'? Does the NCPA reach out to these young ordained children or doesn't it come under their 'purview'? Does the NCPA raise public awareness and influence policies and practices that affect the lives and welfare of these ordained-children as well? Or is it none of their business? Does the NCPA work together with relevant authorities/systems such as the police, healthcare, legal, education, communication, media, political and all sectors of society to look into problems faced by the child *Samaneras* as well? Or don't they care? Does the NCPA contribute to and work towards strengthening and networking with global child protection systems, in ensuring that the voices of these child *Samaneras* are also heard? Or do they not matter? Does the NCPA not regard these ordained children as children of Sri Lanka?

'Sinhala-Buddhist Army' Recruitment Drive

For over 2,500 years, Sri Lanka's Sinhala-Buddhist monks have been wielding significant power over society and the politics of the country. As their strength comes from their numbers, persistent recruitment of 'soldiers' is required to form their power base.

These are times when recruiting adult males to serve their cause has become increasingly challenging. In a society driven by materialism, for most – barring those parasites preferring a free-ride courtesy the tax-payer – ordination is not so attractive. So the only source of recruitment to the Cultural Sinhala-Buddhist Army is to draw young children of gullible or poor parents into their fold. Thus, they secure the continuity of their 'priestly' power.

The unenlightened Sinhala-Buddhist is made to believe that to have one of their own in the Buddhist monkhood is not only meritorious but a matter of great honour and prestige for the family. This is similar to having a son serving the country through the armed forces. In this context, I came across the following news item online:

2550 novice monks to be ordained in Sri Lanka with government assistance

ColomboPage News Desk, 14 November 2006:

Colombo, Sri Lanka   The Sri Lanka Ministry of Education has advised all principal monks of the temple schools, or Pirivenas, to work to fulfill the target of ordaining 2,550 novice monks to commemorate the 2550th anniversary of the passing of the Buddha.

The Director of the temple school branch of the Ministry of Education, Ven. Walaswewe Gnanarathana Thero has issued instructions to the temple schools to ordain novice monks and register them with the Department of Buddhist Affairs. The temples that ordain ten or more such novice monks can open a new temple school with the full assistance of the Government. The Sri Lanka government set the target of ordaining 2550 novice monks to commemorate the 2550th anniversary of the passing of the Buddha, which fell last year. However, fewer parents are agreeing to give up their children for ordination.

"Further, a post-event news item titled 'Mass ordination ceremony in Colombo' appeared in the *Junior Observer* of the government-owned *Sunday Observer* dated 24 June 2007.

Targetted at the junior readership, it would have missed the eye of most adult readers. In an attempt at blatant brainwashing, the author declares enthusiastically to the impressionable young readers of the *Junior Observer*: "The news must have really fascinated you, especially the sight of the Samanera (novice) monks." The *samanera* monks the writer refers to were "in the seven to sixteen age group.

According to these reports, the Cultural Sinhala-Buddhist Rajapaksa Government of Sri Lanka worked hand-in-glove with the Buddhist clergy to "fulfill the target of ordaining 2,550 novice monks, to commemorate the 2,550th anniversary of the passing of the Buddha".

Buddhist Clergy's 'Damaged-Goods'

Philosophical Buddhists have always regarded monks as both the preservers of the Dhamma and its principal exemplars – monks are their spiritual elite. Hence, according to Buddhist monastic rules, one may not be ordained as a fully-ordained monk until twenty years of age. The rationale for this rule is that those under the age of twenty years lack sufficient self-control to live the monastic life.

But the question begs how many of our 'fully-ordained Buddhist monks' above the age of twenty are sufficiently in control of themselves to live according to the monastic code of the Vinaya Pitaka? We have ample evidence of the 'lack', from observing some of the prelates of the 'high caste' Siam Nikaya downwards.

The marauding Gnanasara himself was ordained under the Shyamopoli sub-chapter of the Siam Nikaya at the age of fourteen. Shortly after being ordained, he disrobed, but took robes again at the Kotte Raja Maha Viharaya; another sub-chapter of the Siam Nikaya.

In Sri Lanka, a monk leaving the order is frowned upon by our society and regarded as a 'failure' or even an 'outcast'. The idiomatic term for such an individual is *hiraluva* (ex-monk).

Although highly derogatory, this label has not proved to be a deterrent to many, especially those who take robes for the purpose of enjoying the benefits accorded to Buddhist monks by Sri Lanka's benevolent education system.

In this regard, the Buddha held a very pragmatic view. He expounded that should an ordained person find the monastic life too challenging to sustain, it would be is far wiser for that individual to leave the Order than to break its Vinaya Pitaka and harm both his counterparts as well as himself. However, the likes of Gnanasara care not for the advice of the Buddha and prefer to remain in robes and do what they do, purely because of the power the saffron garment wields.

This is a topic that will not go down well with the Sinhala-Buddhist Culture worshippers of this country, as they consider it 'sacrilegious' to question or denounce any form of wrong committed by any Tom, Dick or Harry swathed in saffron cloth!

However, if their sons are to be the next victims of this insatiable 'recruitment' drive, of 'inducting' the young, unsuspecting and the vulnerable into Sri Lanka's 'Sinhala-Buddhist Army', will they still remain with their heads buried in sand and call it a privilege and an honour?

Sinhala-Buddhism in Sri Lanka

I am a Sri Lankan, Sinhalese, and a follower of Philosophical Buddhism. I absolutely refuse to identify myself as a Sinhala-Buddhist and the Cultural Sinhala-Buddhism that they expound. Why? Because the status quo of the Sinhala-Buddhist identity is associated with all that goes against my principles: bigotry, racial supremacism, hypocrisy and the rest of it that literally stinks and which I find utterly demeaning!

According to the recorded history of this land, it was the 'National Hero', Anagarika Dharmapala (Homeless Protector of the Dhamma), who first espoused the Sinhala-Buddhist identity in pre-independent Ceylon.

Given the socio-political climate of Ceylon at the time, one could appreciate the fact that the Anagarika was rebelling against the most appalling and inhumane treatment the British colonial 'occupants' of our country were subjecting the masses to. But, upon closer examination, the Anagarika's stance against the colonial occupant was obviously not entirely on behalf of all Sri Lankans, but only on behalf of the Sinhala-Buddhists of this country and his ultimate dream of establishing a Sinhala-Buddhist Raj along with the role of historical custodian of Buddhism as perceived in the Mahavamsa.

Although he died fifteen years before British-occupied Ceylon gained independence, he aspired to the eventual emergence of Sri Lanka as a Buddhist nation wherein the 'pristine glory' of his Sinhalese people would flourish – thus sowing the seeds for the 'Mahavamsa mindset' of the Sinhala-Buddhists. Followers of other religious faiths were not included in his equation of a nation. This posture clearly divided the Sinhalese Buddhists of Sri Lanka and the other ethno-religious citizenry of the country.

As such, the Anagarika cannot be regarded as a pristine model of Buddhism who upheld the teachings of the Dhamma. Rather, he was a practitioner of the Mahavamsa. This he vitriolically demonstrated through his chauvinistic rhetorical fire aimed not only at the colonial invaders but at his own countrymen as well. For him Sri Lanka/Ceylon/Dhammadeepa was only for Sinhala-Buddhists and no other!

Thus he donned the mantle of a 'Bodhisattva' and projected himself as the saviour of Buddhism, a task that the Buddha never entrusted him with. He did a bad job of it; instead of spreading the message of the Dhamma preached by the Buddha and leading an exemplary Buddhist life, the Anagarika added his own flavour of nationalism to Buddhism and turned it into a political tool for future use, giving birth to Sinhala-Buddhism!

The Anagarika appears to have suffered from an acute persecution complex regarding the survival of Buddhism in this country, born perhaps out of fear and insecurity of what he and the masses had been subjected to under British occupation. These insecurities have been since passed down generations of Sinhala-Buddhists in Sri Lanka and flourish even today.

The Anagarika's intolerance of the Other was clearly evinced through his customary vitriolic rhetorical fire. He said, "This bright, beautiful island was made into a Paradise by the Aryan Sinhalese before its destruction was brought about by the barbaric vandals. Its people did not know irreligion. ... Christianity and polytheism [i.e. Hinduism] are responsible for the vulgar practices of killing animals, stealing, prostitution, licentiousness, lying and drunkenness . . . The ancient, historic, refined people, under the diabolism of vicious paganism, introduced by the British administrators, are now declining slowly away." Guruge, Ananda. 1965. *Return to Righteousness: A collection of Speeches, Essays and Letters of the Anagarika Dharmapala*, Colombo Ministry of Education and Cultural Affairs.

He also said, "The Muhammedans, an alien people . . . by shylockian methods become prosperous like Jews. The Sinhala sons of the soil, whose ancestors for 2,358 years had shed rivers of blood to keep the country free of alien invaders . . . are in the eyes of the British, only vagabonds. The Alien South Indian Muhammedan come to Ceylon, sees the neglected villager, without any experience in trade . . . and the result is that the Muhammedan thrives and the sons of the sol go to the wall." Jayawardena, Kumari, *Ethnic and Class Conflicts*, pp.29-27

Ultimately, what the Anagarika ended up propagating amongst the Sinhala masses was a chauvinistic ideology flavoured with racism under the banner of Buddhism. By doing so, he sapped the essence of the Dhamma and turned Buddhism into a 'religion' of bigotry and hypocrisy.

What the Rajapaksa regime was aspiring for in Sinhala-Buddhist Sri Lanka was precisely what the Anagarika upheld; a Sinhala-Buddhist nation with a subservient and terrorised Other. Since the majority Cultural Sinhala-Buddhists uphold and worship the Anagarika's Sinhala-Buddhism as opposed to the Buddha's Philosophical Dhamma, would it not be more appropriate to replace all those statues of the Buddha with those of the Anagarika Dharmapala?

Those of us follow the Dhamma do not require perceived images of the Buddha to venerate. We venerate the Dhamma and nothing else!

The Sinhala-Buddhist Political Weapon

In the 1950s, Sinhala-Buddhism took another significant turn. Brandishing Anagarika Dharmapala's Sinhala-Buddhist political weapon, along came S. W. R. D. Bandaranaike, born and buried an Anglican Christian. Throwing scruples to the wind, he transformed himself into a *pro tem* Buddhist to win the hearts and minds of the Sinhala-Buddhist voter base.

Reviving the dormant nationalistic psyche of the gullible Sinhala-Buddhist, brainwashed by 'National Hero' Anagarika Dharmapala, Bandaranaike dived in and resurfaced with this powerful weapon for maximum political mileage. He created mass hysteria under the banner of 'Sinhala-Buddhism', the curse of which continues to plague our nation today. As per his karma, Bandaranaike was gunned down by none other than a pistol-toting Sinhala-Buddhist in saffron robes.

This destructive identity introduced by the Anagarika Dharmapala and propagated by Bandaranaike was to become *sine qua non* for future politicians of Sri Lanka, especially those of his nationalistic Sri Lanka Freedom Party (SLFP), to garner votes at elections. The United National Party (UNP) regarded more as a secular and bourgeoisie party practiced 'Sinhala-Buddhism' in politics more subtly. The late J. R. Jayewardene portrayed himself as a *prima facie* Buddhist and, therefore, never openly referred to the Sinhala-Buddhist identity.

FIGURE 1: TELDUWE SOMARAMA ON THE STEPS OF THE COURTHOUSE, 1962

Source: Author obtained the free media image from the website executed today, published on the web 7 July 2014. Photo credit: A C Alles

FIGURE 2: BUDDHARAKITHA ON THE STEPS OF THE COURTHOUSE, 1962

Source: Author obtained the free media image from the website executed today, published on the web 7 July 2014. Photo credit: A C Alles

His successor, however, the late Ranasinghe Premadasa, turned Sinhala-Buddhism into a drama of sorts. Not satisfied with what Sinhala-Buddhism afforded him, Premadasa went on to embrace Hinduism as well, and reportedly did some other strange things to invoke divine blessings. With this, he set the trend for subsequent politicians to go running to Hindu Gods at various Hindu temples in Sri Lanka and India, and to indulge in rituals such as animal sacrifice, for more and more of whatever they wished for, displaying the basic greed and insecurity of the average primeval human being!

Alas, as depicted in the media, the incumbent Prime Minister, Ranil Wickremesinghe, who many regard as a statesman, appears to have become a victim of this very primitive mindset as well. Bare bodied with ash smeared on his forehead is not a pretty sight of our supposedly-statesman Prime Minister.

The Sinhala Only Act sounded the death knell for a common Sri Lankan identity. This most potent tool of our sociological value system, exacerbated by the accompanying replacement of English as the medium of instruction in schools, tore the ethnic communities apart.

We Sri Lankans, especially the Sinhala-Buddhists, are today nothing but a people with a serious identity crisis. Generations of myopic and selfish politicians are responsible for this. They carried out their deadly political experiments in their laboratory of politics and injected us with various sociologically-toxic viruses that we blindly pass down to successive generations. These virulent viruses have tragically contaminated almost all of our people today. We are no more straightforward Sri Lankans; rather, we are Sinhala-Buddhists, and others, including Sinhala Christians, Tamils, and Muslims etc.

While other countries in the region with a multitude of ethnic groups and religions far more diverse than in Sri Lanka, identify themselves with a single ethnic identity, Sri Lanka continues to fragment itself with ethno-religious identities. Why is the Sinhala-Buddhist so insecure?

I remember a time way back in school, when we didn't know what an ethnic group was. We were all Ceylonese/Sri Lankans in one class: Sinhalese, Tamils, Moors, Burghers, Malays and others. And we were then segregated by ethnic identity. Too young to understand what was going on, all we knew was that we were pulled apart and shoved into classes segregated and based on ethnic identity, for no fault of our own. We were emotionally shattered as our friends had been taken away. Before long, we grew apart. From thereon, we as young children became conscious of our individual ethnicity.

Psychologically, we experienced a growing awareness of our differences. We no longer regarded ourselves as Sri Lankans, but rather as Sinhalese, Tamil or Muslim, etc. Not satisfied with segregating us by ethnicity and language, we were then brainwashed into regarding each other's religion with suspicion.

There are people I know, products of this identity confusion, who have written down their ethno-religious identity as 'Sinhala-Buddhist', instead of their national identity, Sri Lankan, on official documents. Such is their confusion! Never before in recent history have the ethnic communities of this comparatively small island been so polarised. Though physically very close to one another, we are so far apart. Today we are a nation where not only the Sinhalese and Tamils survey each other with fear and suspicion, but the Sinhalese and Muslims do so as well.

Instead of squashing extremism in its infancy, our politicians continue to propagate it in all its ugly forms for their own selfish gains. Do they ever look at the bigger picture and foresee what is to come? Don't they care? Do they ever think of the sacred responsibility of their leadership of our country? Are they so blinded by greed and the spoils that come with it that they will cling to it at any cost? Don't they have a conscience? Are they not patriots?

Is it too much to ask of them to cast aside their myopic and selfish motives, even at this late stage, and unite all as Sri Lankans under one flag?

Requiem for Morals and Ethics

"An established morality is as necessary as good government to the welfare of society. Societies disintegrate from within more frequently than they are broken up by external pressures."

– Judge Patrick Arthur Devlin

Sinhala-Buddhism that has overwhelmingly taken hold of our society has come at great cost to what we Sri Lankans as a nation have become today. With its continued nourishment and protection since independence, the culture of Sinhala-Buddhism has been influencing the political base and dictating State priority, driving the country on a downhill trek. With its near exclusion of Philosophical Buddhism, it has also corrupted the very core of our society in almost every aspect.

The most damaging development has been the increasing supremacism of the Sinhala-Buddhist mindset based on the founding myth in the Mahavamsa. Through its misinterpretation or not as authentic history, the Sinhala majority ethnic community developed a destructive and decisive superiority complex. With the majority adopting this frame of mind, a degenerative disease struck.

The Rajapaksa regime embraced the near-mediaeval ethos of ancient kingdoms of Lanka with gusto. At the helm, Mahinda Rajapaksa appeared to regard himself as the modern-day Dutugamunu, ruler of Sinhala-Buddhist Sri Lanka. He turned the bureaucracy into his private and personal bandwagon of slaves at his command. Like Dutugamunu, he used the Buddhist religion – the opium of the masses – to gain and remain in power. And there were willing champions among the Buddhist clergy to cheer him on.

A culture of corruption, nepotism, fraud, inefficiency and indiscipline coupled with a lack of accountability, rule of law, courtesy and respect for other religions reduced to levels of absurdity, became the hallmark of the Rajapaksa 'Sinhala-Buddhist kingdom'. This decay of societal morals and values today can be directly attributed to the Rajapaksa legacy, which has pervaded our social structure almost in its entirety; from the lowest ranks of employment to the highest of academia!

The Cultural Sinhala-Buddhist clergy have not been immune to the malaise. Despite the pious façade of the saffron robe, their base instincts – the subconscious urge based on primeval self-serving and ignoble motivations such as greed and selfishness ingrained in the human psyche – surfaced in the face of the Other. What humiliation this is for a country marketed internationally as the 'cradle of Theravada Buddhism'!

Thus, hoodwinked first-time visitors to this resplendent land may be pardoned if they expect to see our Buddhist monks suspended in midair with halos above their heads. However, instead of men of pious sobriety, they are more likely to see the likes of Gnanasara and his ilk running amok. No wonder these monks keep hitting world headlines, humiliating and disgracing the image of Buddhism and Buddhists in Sri Lanka.

The reality behind this facade of holiness is a much-depraved society manifesting all its ugliness and making obvious the stark absence of an established morality and thus compassion in a country associated with Buddhism. Much like the clichéd '2,500-year-old culture' of this land, which remains today only in the form of ruins of ancient monuments and edifices, so is our moral culture in ruins!

The seemingly ceaseless propensity towards moral degeneration is all around us today. Not a day goes by without reports of murder, rape, child abuse, thuggery, drug-abuse related offences, sexual harassment of women, antics of corrupt-to-the-core politicians, the police, and even some in academia. Most often these even make it to the headlines.

In a society driven by greed for material wealth and power at any cost, morality holds no water. Even once highly respected and revered professions such as medicine, law, education and the media are now infected with those morally bankrupt and caught up in the destructive trap of greed. Where do we now look for examples to emulate?

The few who continue to uphold morals are trodden on by the depraved. Their voices are ignored, unheard or silenced, and they are thus unable to turn the tide of the moral collapse of our society.

The Once-Hallowed Fourth Estate

As a journalist with more than thirty seven years of experience in print and electronic media, I would like to cite as an example of what has become of our once-hallowed institution – the Fourth Estate. I feel for and lament the death of what many of us journalists prized the most: media ethics, the absence of which today is a reminder of how things used to be.

I recall times not too long ago when only the refined and cultured, were drawn to this noble profession. Financial benefits, rewards and remuneration did not matter to them. Most often than not they were even out of pocket. Back then, to be a member of the erudite Fourth Estate was an honour and a privilege. Journalists were respected, looked up to, and almost revered by the reading, listening and viewing public. They upheld democracy and the responsibility of fair, unbiased, honest, accurate and accountable reporting and writing while abiding by sacrosanct media ethics. They required no formal grounding in ethics either, as it was ingrained in their breeding and persona.

Back then, a professional journalist wouldn't dream of selling his/her soul for the 'right price', by availing their services, not only to expose but also to tarnish the image of others or cover-up or shield the ugly and corrupt. The very thought of reducing the noble Fourth Estate to a level which would make the world's oldest profession appear respectable, was tantamount to sacrilege in their eyes.

Back then, the revered title of 'editor' was reserved only for the crème de la crème of the Fourth Estate, who encompassed all that was cultured and honourable in the profession; refinement of the mind, morals and taste. They never used the media they headed to buttress their overinflated egos. Nor would they stoop to such lows as to use it as a weapon to be wielded for personal vendetta or blackmail. My first boss and mentor the late Rex De Silva, the Editor in Chief of the *Sun* and *Weekend* newspapers, was a beacon of this noble culture!

Today journalism has become the 'profession' of any Tom, Dick and Harry looking for a regular income, through fair means or foul. Commitment to professionalism, the upholding of media ethics and standards are stark in their absence. And the handful of the few who continue to uphold such ethics and morality are lost amidst a mélange of the other kind.

It is said that whenever Napoleon conquered a country, his first step was to take control of the main media of his time; the newspapers. What we see happening in Sri Lanka today is no different, except the term 'media', encompasses a much wider area than in Napoleon's time.

Our media – newspapers, radio, television and social media – are now controlled and manipulated by powerful forces not limited to the government in power. Information dished out to the public is slanted, distorted, sensationalised and spurious 'realities' are manufactured to suit personal agendas. Photographs and television camera angels are used to 'sanitize' and praise the corrupt and to denigrate, ridicule and scorn the honest, and are no longer a reflection of reality.

It is true that those who control the media, control the mind. With the most powerful propaganda tool mobilised to further the agendas of the powerful, the masses are constantly bombarded and brainwashed by pseudo-realities manufactured by the unscrupulous.

A country's media is a reflection of its society!

Epilogue

Memories of certain incidents and words heard when I was just a child have remained with me to date. One was the shocking and repugnant practice of caste segregation upheld by none other than the prelates of the Sinhala-Buddhist religious establishment. The second was a conversation with my late maternal grandfather, Justice Walter Thalgodapitiya, famed for his 'Thalgodapitiya Commission Report'.

Barely in my teens, I did not attach much importance to his words at the time. Yet, they must have had quite an impact on my psyche for I recall them even today. During that conversation, he referred to a rock inscription somewhere in Sri Lanka, I can't recall where, which prophesied that Sri Lanka would one day be ruled by a 'slit-eyed' race. While it sounded ridiculous at the time, it doesn't seem so anymore!

Today, the morale of the people of Sri Lanka have fallen to a dangerous low. Successive governments, voted in by trusting masses, have let us down in one way or another. We are a nation of people sad, tired and disappointed, without hope and extremely vulnerable. We know we need a change in the system to put things right. But how?

Meanwhile, just as a potentially harmful virus can take over and destroy one with a weak immune system, a slit-eyed race is gradually taking over the country. Do we have the strength or the will to stop them? A few of us do, but is that enough?

We belong to the Democratic Socialist Republic of Sri Lanka. Yet, how well has democracy served us? Democracy in this country has been and continues to be used and abused top down; from our politicians to the masses who are too immature and uneducated to appreciate and value it.

I firmly believe that democracy hasn't and never will work in Sri Lanka, at least not at present. We are still too immature. Sri Lanka gained independence too soon and the politicians who stepped in after the British led us down the garden path. Their descendants continue to do so.

For democracy to function, this country needs a thorough cleanup; firstly, of all its virulent ills, starting with our multi-party Members of Parliament unworthy of representing the people, and those doddering, who will soon be pushing daisies, retained for party loyalty.

This is where the rot started and began spreading its tentacles. Today the judiciary is infected, having lost sight of morality; the law enforcement mechanism is unable to maintain the rule of law; and a self-serving academia has become puppets in the hands of politicians with personal agendas. Even religious establishments, starting with the Buddhist monks, have not been spared!

Religion, which is a private and personal matter, and the history of this country based mostly on myth and allegory, must be eliminated from the school curricula. What good have they done so far except to brainwash and polarise the masses?

As repeated by many before me, what Sri Lanka direly needs is a visionary leader of the likes of Lee Kuan Yew and Mahathir bin Mohamad. Under the current multi-party, political system, no politician will have the guts to take the bull by the horns and put things right for fear of losing votes, save for one!

If all fails, we can look forward to the looming slit-eyed sword of Damocles sever our heads and we will have no option but, seek refuge in the Indian Ocean along with our 'glorious' 2,500-year-old culture!

Ingram Content Group UK Ltd.
Milton Keynes UK
UKHW011835140323
418553UK00001B/92